A History of

HIGHLAND LOCOMOTIVES

A History of HIGHLAND LOCOMOTIVES

by Peter Tatlow

based on the original book by M.C.V. Allchin

Oxford Publishing Co. Oxford

First published in 1947

Revised and extended edition 1979

SBN 86093 048 3

Printed by B. H. Blackwell
in the City of Oxford

Published by
Oxford Railway Publishing Co. Ltd.,
8 The Roundway,
Headington,
Oxford.

Frontispiece:
A view of Inverness station from the east in the early 1900s showing the events leading up to the departure of the 3.50 pm for the south behind a 4–4–0 'Loch' and 4–6–0 'Castle' class locomotives. On the left 4–4–0 'Small Ben' No. 47 ***Ben a' Bhuird*** has just arrived with the connecting train from the north, having traversed the Ross Street curve behind Lochgorm Works to the right and reversed into the station. In the centre is station pilot 4–4–0T 'Jones Tank' No. 58 ***Burghead***.
(P. Tatlow collection)

CONTENTS

Plate 1

Lochgorm Works (P. Tatlow)

PREFACE TO FIRST EDITION

In presenting what is believed to be the most complete summary of Highland locomotives yet published, the author has endeavoured to include detailed information of every locomotive which came into the possession of the Highland Railway, from its incorporation until its final absorption. To include all the information which came to hand would have necessitated a book several times the size of this volume. Nevertheless, it is thought that the details herein will prove adequate for most readers. Whilst every effort has been made to ensure accuracy it is too much to hope that no errors will be found in a work of this magnitude. Furthermore, well-known authorities give different versions in many instances, the records given here are either officially confirmed or else the result of careful scrutiny of all available evidence. Renumbering and renaming was particularly rife on this railway, with consequent added difficulty to the historian. Although the Highland Railway was not incorporated until 1865, the history will be found to include a full list of locomotives of all the earlier constituent companies, the largest of which was the Inverness & Aberdeen Junction Railway. A table is included at the end of the book outlining these companies in chronological order, together with subsequent absorptions. Likewise, although the Highland Company ceased to exist in 1922, withdrawal dates are included right up to 1947. At the time of writing, the locomotive stock has dwindled to 31 tender and 2 tank engines, a total of 33, as compared with 55 in 1865 and 173 in 1922, the latter figure being the highest ever attained. Whilst a complete stock list for any individual year is readily derived, those for the years 1865, 1922 and 1947 being of particular interest are set out in full. Annual totals of all types also provide interesting comparisons.

Locomotives are listed in the class and type of their original construction and are identified by their original running number. Subsequent changes may be traced onwards from that point. The date of LMSR renumbering is that of the numbering allocations, the actual renumbering took some years to complete. Rebuilding, involving a change of wheel-type will be indicated specifically, in other cases references may be limited to rebuilding of complete classes. It should be noted that the tender and tank engine summaries, given at the end of the respective sections, do not take note of rebuilding. Thus the 31 2–4–0s listed are all original 2–4–0s and do not include those which were rebuilt from 2–2–2s, the latter having already appeared in the 2–2–2 total. Likewise the tank summary makes no mention of a 2–2–2T since the engine in question was a rebuild of a different type.

In compiling these records the author has been involved in a good deal of correspondence and is indebted to numerous writers for information ranging from odd dates to detailed lists. Others have gone to some trouble to hunt up old references or sort out old photographs, and their help has been invaluable. In order that any future editions may be made even more complete the author would welcome any further information, or details as to the whereabouts of existing photographs or drawings of locomotives not illustrated. In this connection it was thought desirable to include as many line drawings as possible in order to assist the model railway enthusiasts who have the Highland Railway as their prototype.

In conclusion the author pays grateful acknowledgements to the numerous correspondents who have contributed information, and particularly to W.E. Beckerlegge, Esq., for detailed checking and helpful suggestions; to K.H. Leech, Esq., for the use of many of his line drawings; to the Stephenson Locomotive Society for the loan of the line blocks; to H.C. Casserley, Esq., for his many excellent photographs; to F. Moore (Locomotive Publishing Co., Ltd.) for an excellent photographic collection of locomotives in Highland livery; to J.F. McEwan, Esq., for the loan of photographs; to A.W. Croughton, Esq., for photographs; and to the North British Locomotive Co., Ltd., for checking and supplying information. Acknowledgements are also due to ***The Locomotive, The Railway Magazine*** and the Journal of the Stephenson Locomotive Society, and to earlier writers, H.A. Vallance, Esq., C. Hamilton Ellis, Esq., and the late E.L. Ahrons, Esq. For access to earlier reference works, now out of print, the writer is indebted to the services of the City of Portsmouth Public Library, who successfully traced copies and arranged for their loan. Finally, by courtesy of the London, Midland & Scottish Railway Company and the kindness of G.S. Bellamy, Esq., of St. Rollox Works, Glasgow, to whom the author is greatly indebted, the manuscript was officially checked, many items of missing information being added at the same time. In certain instances, notably dates of withdrawal, renumbering and renaming, official confirmation was not always available, but something like ninety-five per cent. of the information listed may be regarded as official.

M.C.V. ALLCHIN

Fareham.
June, 1947.

PREFACE TO SECOND EDITION

An affection for Highland locomotives and a desire to make them more widely known has led me to approach the original author of ***A history of Highland locomotives*** and my publisher with a view to reprinting a revised and extended edition. That my request met with their approval is evidenced by this book and I am grateful to them both for the opportunity to present again the details, drawings and photographs of these magnificent locomotives.

My own introduction to Scottish railways began at an early and impressionable age when during the blitz of World War II my mother removed my younger brother and me from the county of Surrey to the safer refuge of the Isle of Bute on the west coast of Scotland. But it was not until a few years later during the summer of 1945 on the train journey south from Oban, following a holiday on the Isle of Mull, that I had a named engine pointed out to me which I believe to have been a Highland locomotive. To this day I do not know which one, although I suspect it was a 'Clan' and apart from No. 103 remains the only HR locomotive I ever spotted.

Military service ten years later offered the opportunity to use one's travel warrant to advantage and an overnight sleeper journey from Euston to Inverness, followed by the trip out to Kyle of Lochalsh aroused my dormant interests in the railways of Scotland. When shortly afterwards while browsing through a second hand bookshop outside Waterloo station I came across ***A history of Highland locomotives*** by M.C.V. Allchin, it was a foregone conclusion that I should part with ten shillings and really come to terms with the engines that manfully struggled to provide the Highlands with railway communications.

At the time that this little book first appeared soon after the War, such a production represented a substantial achievement and was the beginnings of a growing and developing line of publications for the railway enthusiast. It is only proper therefore that we should return to this book and re-present it in the manner to which we have become accustomed and in a sense expand it in the way that the original author might have wished from the outset had circumstances permitted.

Some criticism of the first edition was raised to the effect that it did not live up to the word ***history*** in its title and, whilst readers will find that this revision includes some fresh material, it is still not a definitive history in the sense that it does not include every minutia, nor try to establish the background to some of the more controversial events that took place during the period under review. On the other hand much additional data has been added mainly in the form of tables in the appendices and an outline of the liveries applied to these engines; although in the case of the latter it is hoped that by the time this book appears in print a full livery register of all aspects of the Highland railway may have been published.

The emphasis of this book will be on the pictorial aspects of Highland locomotives in their historical context. In the first edition Mr. Allchin says that the line drawings were provided primarily for the benefit of modellers and since then increasing attention has been directed by this fraternity to obtaining reliable prototype information. As a modeller myself I hope therefore that the reproduction of most drawings at the commonly used scale of 4 mm to 1 foot, the inclusion wherever possible of end views and some plans, together with dimensions, will encourage a growing number to build for themselves accurate models of this interesting group of locomotives.

In compiling this revised edition I have been helped by numerous people and organisations, some of whom were associated with the original work. My thanks are due to them all, for without their assistance which is noted in the acknowledgements, this edition could never have appeared.

Peter Tatlow 1979

Plate 2

GENERAL REVIEW

EARLIEST LOCOMOTIVES

The ancestors to all Highland Railway locomotives were to be found in the two 2–2–2 tender engines purchased by the Inverness and Nairn Railway (I & NR) from Hawthorn & Co. of Leith, once a subsidiary of Hawthorns of Newcastle-upon-Tyne, in time for the introduction of their train services between those two northern Scottish towns in November 1855. Gradually this railway was extended, first in 1858 to Elgin and Keith under the title of the Inverness and Aberdeen Jct. Rly. (I & AJR), to meet the Great North of Scotland (GNSR) from Aberdeen, and for which a further two engines of similar design were acquired. Whilst the six foot diameter single wheelers may have been adequate for the light traffic experienced initially, as this developed something with greater pulling power was required especially to handle goods trains and to this end seven 2–4–0s with five foot diameter coupled wheels were obtained in 1858 from the builders Hawthorn of Leith.

These lines expanded northwards in 1862 with the Inverness and Ross-shire Railway to Dingwall and Invergordon a year later and culminating with the mighty Inverness and Perth Jct. Rly's (I & PJR) through route over the Grampians in 1863; leading to further batches of 2–2–2s and 2–4–0s being delivered to the I & AJR. Although in most cases set up as nominally independent companies, each seeking and obtaining an Act of Parliament authorising the construction of its stretch of line, it is clear from the names frequently reappearing among the promoters that there was some overall strategic direction with the intention of providing railway communication to the northern parts of Scotland. The various companies that amalgamated to form the Highland Railway in 1865 and the subsequent ones set up to extend the line to the west and further north, all of which eventually came into the Highland fold, are shown as a tree in figure 1 with their dates of opening to traffic and amalgamation.

HIGHLAND RAILWAY GENEAOLOGY

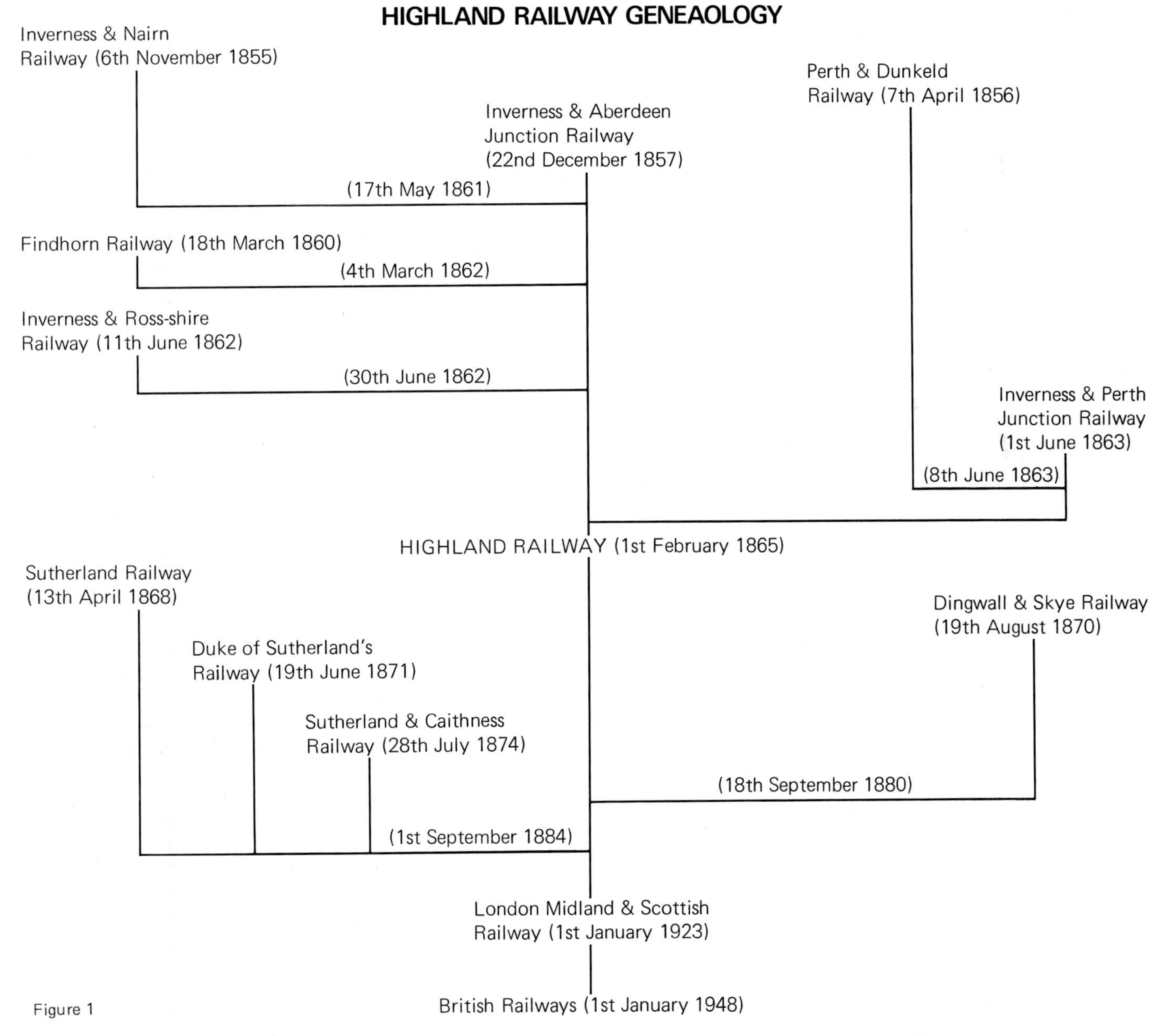

Figure 1

Figure 2

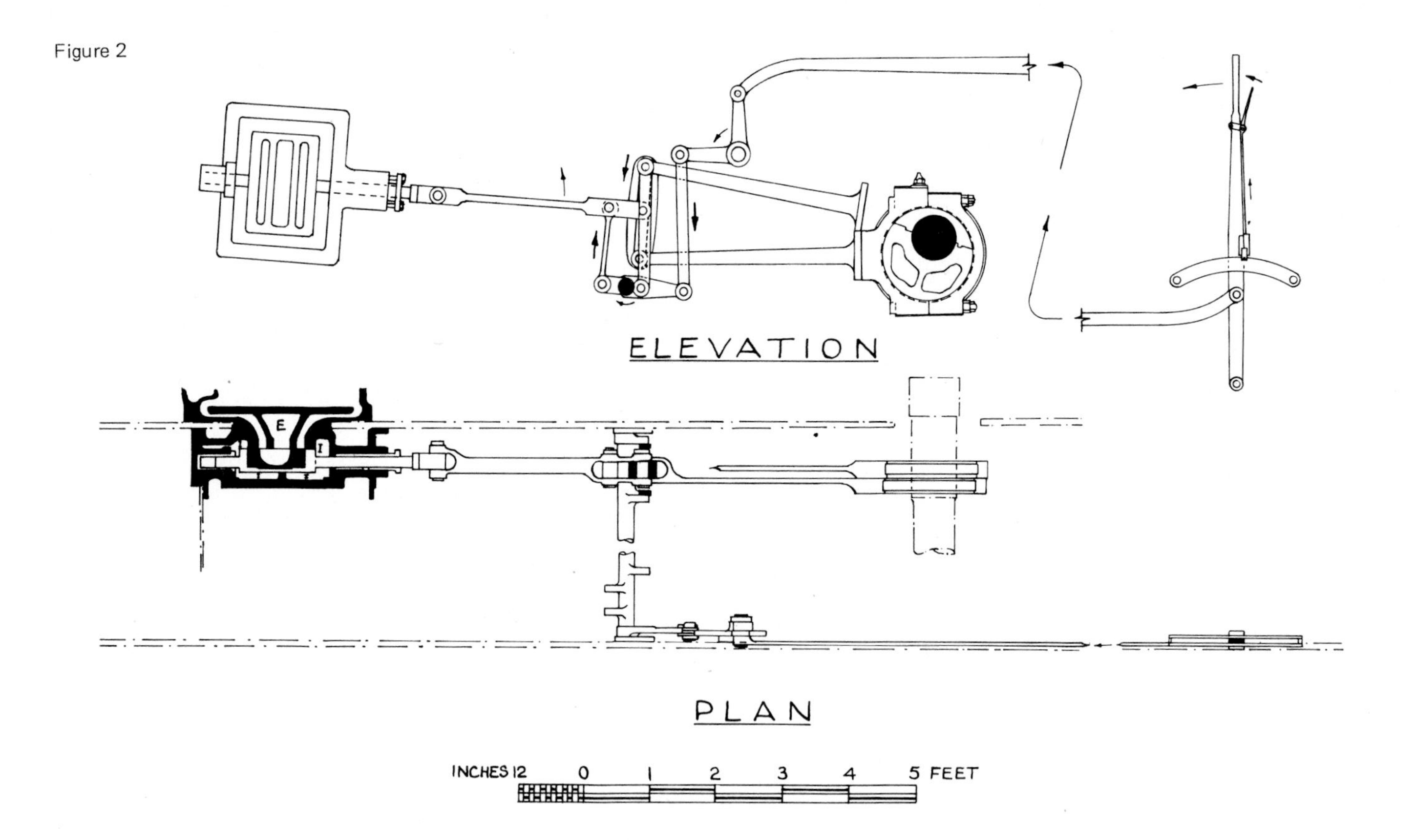

ALEXANDER ALLAN

A major moving spirit in the direction and execution of these railway constructions was Joseph Mitchell, Engineer to all the early companies and amongst other things it was he who was to recommend to the I & NR Board of Directors Alexander Allan, the then recently appointed Locomotive Superintendent of the Scottish Central Railway and formerly Foreman of Locomotives at Crewe, to undertake the design and supervision of the construction of the first locomotives for the I & NR and, with only two isolated exceptions, all further locomotives for the constituents of the Highland Railway up until the amalgamation of 1865. Therefore from the outset a reasonably similar stud of locomotives was brought into use as listed in appendix 1 and in later pages an outline of their development will be given.

Allan is perhaps best remembered for his straight link motion which at a time when machine tools were in their infancy was easier to manufacture than the well known Stephenson curved link motion and gave satisfactory valve events. This gear, which was introduced in 1855 and was fitted to all the engines built under his direction for the Highland companies, is illustrated in figure 2. His inventive and thoroughly practical mind was turned to many problems in locomotive design and he presented papers to the Institution of Mechanical Engineers, to which he was elected a member in 1847, on such diverse subjects as boilers, pressure gauges, oil lubricated axles, steam brakes and feed pipe connections, as well as his straight link valve motion, together with one on gas meters.

It is perhaps easily forgotten a century or more later that at these times the process of burning coal in a locomotive firebox to obtain complete combustion had not been fully evolved and many railways were instead still using more expensive coke as a fuel, because it was more or less smokeless. Several of Allan's classes incorporated a variety of firebox designs with either longitudinal or transverse mid-feathers and double doors of the Beattie or variations on the Beattie type. It was only with the advent of the brick arch in the firebox that a satisfactory means of burning coal in locomotives was established.

The details and visual appearance of Allan designed locomotives built for the Highland companies were in every way of the Crewe tradition. All the features of outside cylinders between double framing eliminating the need for the then suspect crank axle, solid 'big ends', smokeboxes with the plating swept round the cylinders in a reverse curve, raised fireboxes, outside bearings to the leading and trailing axles, Salter spring balance safety valves and piston type regulator were incorporated. Anyone doubting the close connections of these early I & NR and I & AJR locomotives and the contemporary products of Crewe should compare the illustrations in the following pages with ***Columbine*** built in 1845 at Crewe, now installed in the National Railway Museum at York, making allowance for the cab which is a later addition and the chimney which is not original.

Initially the locomotivemen were merely provided with a forward weather sheet with lookouts and low sides of thin gauge sheeting between stanchions and a capping rail. However, by 1862 with the delivery of Nos 12 and 13 of the 'Belladrum' class the stanchions were extended to a cant rail supporting a roof in the form of an arc transversely but also shaped in a curve to the straight front edge. This type of cab roof is sometimes attributed to Stroudley, who reproduced it in considerable numbers on the London, Brighton and South Coast Railway (LBSC), but clearly it predates his sojourn at Inverness.

To attend to the day to day running of the locomotives, Allan appointed his nephew William Barclay to be Locomotive Superintendent at Inverness in August 1855. It should not be presumed from the title of this post that he was in any way responsible for the design of these locomotives, but merely to supervise their maintenance. A task which as the numbers of engines grew he failed to carry out to the satisfaction of the Directors of the newly formed Highland Railway. Following an incident when he was seen by Colonel Fraser-Tytler fishing by the lineside while traffic was suffering serious delays due to an engine failure, he was given notice of the termination of his employment from 31st May, 1865.

WILLIAM STROUDLEY

On the appointment of William Stroudley in June that year it seems he was given a wider responsibility than his predecessor Barclay. With the completion of the deliveries the previous year of Allan designed locomotives for the main line to Perth, the system was adequately stocked and Allan's connection with the railway also ceased. Stroudley was only given the opportunity to design one locomotive for the company and even that made use of a cut down boiler from one of the earliest Allan single wheelers. However, these Lochgorm built tanks were significant, two more being added by Stroudley's successor after his departure to the LBSC in January, 1870, where he himself went on to develop it into his well known 0–6–0T 'Terrier' class. In addition it was under his direction that the first of the single wheelers No. 1 ***Raigmore*** was rebuilt as a 2–4–0, which while not entirely successful due to weak frames led to all but one of the large class of later Allan single wheelers being rebuilt in a similar fashion.

DAVID JONES

This time David Jones, the young man who had very briefly held the reins between Barclay's and Stroudley's tenure of office, was on 25th January, 1870 given permanent charge of affairs at Lochgorm, the company's works at Inverness, and he was to continue in this post for the next twenty six years. Jones was an Englishman who, following an apprenticeship under John Ramsbottom, came to Inverness at the time of the opening of the I & NR and quickly established his worth under Barclay and Stroudley. His initial work was to continue Stroudley's first steps at improving the Allan single wheelers. In the second conversion of one of the I & NR engines No. 2 ***Aldourie***, new frames and boiler were provided and serviceable parts added, Nos 3 and 4 being cannibalised to provide the second pair of driving wheels. As already noted the boiler of No. 3 was used on Stroudley's six coupled tank engine No. 56 and Jones put No. 4 and 1's boilers on the second and third engines of this class, Nos 57 and 16 respectively.

Financially times were difficult in the early 1870s and therefore the slow process of improving the existing stock continued with one or occasionally two singles being converted every year until 1884. On the whole the 2–4–0s were more suited to their work as built, but they benefited from enlarged cylinders, the fitting of which again was undertaken gradually over the years.

Mr Jones' appointment had stipulated that his responsibilities were to include the locomotives required to operate the Dingwall and Skye Railway about to open to the then terminus at Strome Ferry on Loch Carron. Actually no new engines were delivered at this time and the small wheeled 2–4–0s were at first used. However, it is reported that their rigid wheel base caused problems on the sharp curves of the line and within three years No. 7 had been provided with a bogie of the Adams' type, which permitted some lateral displacement at the leading end. It may not have been insignificant that the neighbouring GNSR had been using this wheel arrangement since 1862. No. 7 evidently proving successful, No. 10 was similarly taken in hand two years later. At this distance in time it is strange to think that a rigid wheelbase of 14 ft 3 in should have caused difficulty, when we now know the LMS Stanier 4–6–0 5P5F, commonly known as 'Black 5s', with a coupled wheelbase of 15 ft 4 in worked the line for more than twenty years without apparent problems including the more sinuous extension of the line around the rocky coast from Strome Ferry to Kyle of Lochalsh opened in 1897. The only mitigating factors may have been that an improved wheel tyre profile with reduced flange depth was adopted by the railways of Britain during the second decade of this century and the development of a better understanding of curve alignment and the means of maintaining realigned curves under traffic.

The forced adoption of the 4–4–0 wheel arrangement showed the way of things to come until almost the end of Mr Jones' tenure of office. His first new engines and the first entirely new engines for the Highland Railway were the ten 'Duke' class built by Dübs of Glasgow in 1874. In the years following the Highland Railway slowly added to the class by constructing further examples at their own Lochgorm Works. Minor changes were made to the boiler and tender, but the machinery remained unaltered. In 1886 the newly formed Clyde Locomotive Co. of Glasgow supplied eight more known as 'Clyde Bogies' and six years later a significant increase in boiler size was provided on the twelve locomotives of the 'Strath' class. Concurrent with these developments a return had been made to the original conception of a small wheeled four coupled bogie locomotive especially for use on the Skye road, when a

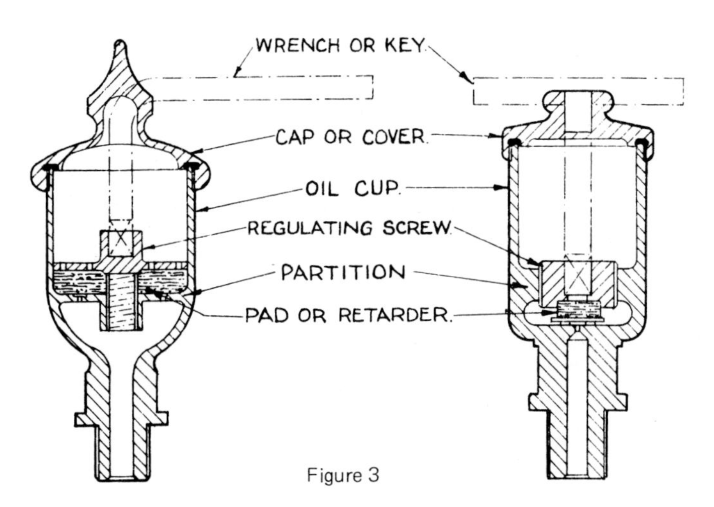

Figure 3

new engine again with the same machinery as the 'Duke' class was built at Lochgorm in 1882: although it was to be another ten years before this design was multiplied to become the famous 'Skye Bogie' class.

In 1874 Jones patented his lubricator that subsequently was to become such a familiar sight usually mounted centrally on the cylinder wrapping, although in later years some appear to have been moved to the front of the smokebox. Its purpose was to provide a uniform flow of oil to the cylinders. This was achieved, as shown in figure 3, by placing oil in the cup which finds its way through holes in the disc into the gauze pad, where it becomes mixed with steam, is drawn through further holes in the lower chamber and on into the cylinder. The flow could be regulated by adjusting the tightness of the disc bearing on the gauze by turning a wrench inserted through the cup, thereby causing the disc to be screwed in or out and incidentally removed for cleaning and replacement of the gauze.

The 'Duke' and 'Clyde Bogie' classes were also provided with the simple equipment necessary to enable them to use counterpressure steam for braking in the manner propounded by M. Le Chatelier. This French engineer realised that if steam and water from the boiler were introduced into the exhaust side of the cylinders and later hot water alone was found to be satisfactory, the usual objections to reversing a locomotive while in motion could be overcome. Instead of hot gases from the smokebox, a fine mist of water was drawn into the cylinders and compressed, thereby raising its temperature sufficiently to convert it into steam and even superheat it, after which the reverse action of the pistons forced it into the boiler. The driver was provided with a small valve in the backplate by which he was able to admit a controlled quantity of water into the exhaust steam pipe, before reversing his gear and leaving the regulator open. By adjusting the valve sufficient water could be allowed in to cause a light water vapour to be emitted from the blast pipe, thus ensuring that only vapour was entering the cylinders, whilst braking was controlled by the reverser. The water vapour in the cylinders provided the necessary lubrication to the slide valves, the cylinder walls and gland packing and by preventing the entry of flue gases into the boiler kept the contents pure and enabled the injectors to function as normal.

This method of braking clearly had its advantages on a line with lengthy gradients such as the Highland, where the more controlled retardation greatly reduced wear to brake blocks, wheels and rail head: whilst the heat generated by reducing the train's kinetic energy was put to useful purpose rather than being wasted. In the days when braking was by means of hand brakes on the tender and a few brake vans within the train or Newall's chain brake with which the Highland lines had been equipped since 1863: it had much to commend it, even if it demanded a skill in application more usually associated with the French ***mécanicien*** than his British counterpart. Although one can see the reason for applying the system to the 'Duke' class in 1874, by 1886 when the 'Clyde Bogies' were built with vacuum brake as standard equipment, the advantage is less obvious. It was also considered preferable to have screw operated reversers, whereas all Highland locomotives at this time were lever worked. Strangely enough a not dissimilar system had briefly been tried by F Holt on the South Staffordshire Railway, but following an accident when the reverser lever slipped into forward gear the experiment was terminated.

In his final years as Locomotive Superintendent David Jones continued to show his ability to put his confidence in worthwhile advances in design to meet the traffic demands of the day placed on his department. No reminder is needed of the significance of the introduction of his 'Big Goods', the first engine of 4–6–0 wheel arrangement in Britain. Although a number of breaks with the Crewe tradition were made with the abandonment of the double framing and cylinders enveloped in the swept out smokebox wrapper, the design represented a carefully thought out continuing line of development. The bold step was not so much that a 4–6–0 wheel arrangement was tried, but that fifteen were ordered by a small railway company straight off the drawing board. That this was justified is exemplified by the success the engines achieved in traffic and the fame that attended them.

The same confidence was shown when an order was placed again for fifteen locomotives of the 'Loch' class in 1896. Of 4–4–0 wheel arrangement for passenger traffic, initially on the main line from Perth to Inverness, including the soon to be completed direct route from Aviemore to Inverness via Slochd summit, the boiler showed only a small increase in size over the previous 'Strath' class, but the cylinders were greater in diameter by one inch. Unfortunately the faith placed in one innovation incorporated in this design, namely the piston valves of W M Smith patent, was shown in a short while to be ill-founded and Jones' successor replaced them with Richardson balanced slide valves.

It is known that Jones foresaw the potential of the 4–6–0 wheel arrangement as an express passenger locomotive and schemed out such a design. It must have been a cruel blow to him that an injury sustained while running trials with a 'Big Goods' locomotive should lead to his resigning his position in 1896, thereby leaving it to his successor to put the finishing touches to the design which as the 'Castle' class first appeared in 1900.

The high regard with which David Jones was held by his men is exemplified by Murdoch Finlayson, a driver who had started on the Skye line in 1903, and who was moved to write of the 'Skye Bogies' and 'Castles':

> 'No subsequent classes, whether Highland, LMS or British Railways ever equalled these classes in reliability, haulage, speed and gradient work . . .'

Praise indeed!

On a more serious note the workings of the Highland Railway demanded first class locomotives of high haulage power and it is therefore no accident that the 'Duke' class was at the time of its introduction the most powerful locomotive in the country and other Highland designs were frequently at the head of their field in this respect. It speaks volumes for Jones' work that twenty years after his retirement one of his designs the 'Lochs' and another of his conceptions the 'Castles' should be chosen for further production to help the company out of a locomotive crisis.

Another aspect of his work which seems to have been overlooked in the past is the forethought that went into his designs from the point of view of future maintenance. E J H Lemon, Vice-President of LMS, had gained much of his early running shed experience at Inverness and later was to speak in the highest terms of Jones' almost unrecognised pioneering work on standardisation of parts amongst similar classes and the ease with which these could be stripped down and replaced, hence reducing cost and the time the engine was out of service. Both of course were valuable assets to the Highland, especially the latter during the summer rush of traffic. Comparison of his earlier designs of 4–4–0 will show much in common and again between his 'Big Goods' and 'Loch' classes. On top of this the design of the boilers was excellent and when after many years maintenance was necessary they were readily accessible and easy to work on.

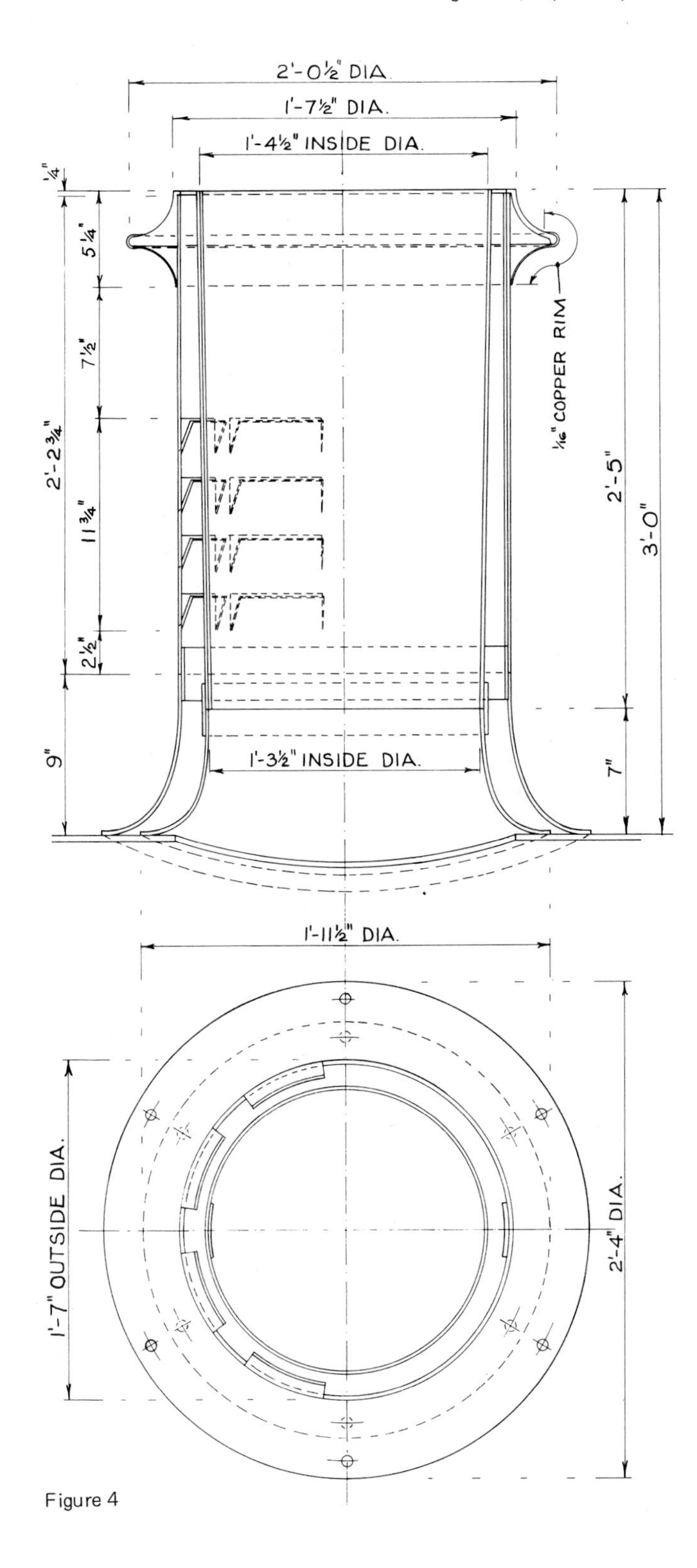

Figure 4

The style of David Jones' locomotives was very much in the Crewe tradition and on the Highland this was probably developed more than on any other railway with the possible exception of the North London. Whereas Stroudley had taken the earlier cab one stage by eliminating the stanchions within the sheeting and sweeping in the rear splashers, Jones adopted the curve between the front and side sheets and almost square front window with rounded lower corner adjacent to the boiler so characteristic of his designs. Another speciality was the louvred chimney consisting of a double wall with an annular chamber closed at the bottom and open at the top, the outer wall being louvred on the forward half and the whole capped with a polished copper rim, as shown in figure 4. Debate rages as to its purpose, some saying that it was to lift the exhaust in windy conditions frequently encountered in the northern latitudes clear of the driver's line of sight, while others are of the opinion that by throwing the hot cinders higher this increased the chance of their cooling before reaching the ground, an equally important consideration in view of the extensive tracts of woodland adjacent to so many of the Highland's lines.

PETER DRUMMOND

To take over from David Jones the Board of the Highland Railway obtained the services of Peter Drummond, until then Assistant Works Manager for the Caledonian Railway at St Rollox and younger brother of the better known Dugald Drummond, successively Locomotive Superintendent to the North British, Caledonian and London & South Western railways and himself for three years a Works Manager of Lochgorm under Stroudley.

Whilst his predecessor had first to rebuild the Allan locomotives and subsequently develop improved designs to meet the needs of the increasing traffic on the main line, the earlier engines long since relegated to secondary services were now reaching the end of their useful lives. Drummond's first task therefore was to provide replacements for the 'Glenbarries' with the 4–4–0 'Ben' class introduced in 1898 for passenger haulage, seventeen of which were in service by 1901, followed by three more in 1906. For the freight side the same boiler, firebox and cylinders were placed on a six-coupled tender locomotive, ten of which had been supplied by 1902 and a further two in 1907.

Although it was only during the summer of 1896 that Jones had placed the fifteen 'Lochs' in service, within four years the logical passenger engine development of his 'Big Goods' was put into production by Drummond. The outside cylinders, Allan valve gear, flangeless middle driving wheels and firebox mounted direct loaded column type safety valves of these 4–6–0 'Castle' class suggest Jones' influence. On the other hand the chimney, bogie, steam reverser, marine type 'big ends', cab and the cumbersome bogie tender with inside bearings are no doubt attributable to Drummond. Again by 1902 a total of ten locomotives to this latest design were in use and the addition of these three classes enabled the majority of the remaining Allan locomotives and even Jones' 'Duke' class to be withdrawn and broken up during the ensuing years.

Some of the parts recovered from these engines including three new boilers were in 1903 reassembled into three six-coupled tank engines. Intended for shunting duties they had somewhat large wheels for this purpose. For branch line service four diminutive 0–4–4Ts were built new at Lochgorm, the last of which was the final new locomotive constructed at the Company's Works, although overhauls were to continue there until after nationalisation.

In 1908 larger boilers were supplied to a fresh series of four 'Ben' class locomotives, known officially as the 'New Ben' class, although more usually referred to as the 'Big Ben' to distinguish them from the 'Small' or 'Wee Bens'. Two more were added the following year.

Although heavy trains had been piloted or banked, or even both, over the steeper gradients from the outset of operations, it was not until 1909 that Drummond in his last design for the Highland built engines for such a purpose. Locomotive designers were now entering the decade of the big tank and the ensuing 0–6–4T was certainly big for the Highland, even if other railways were to have even larger machines. Based on the six-coupled goods engines with a shorter coupled wheelbase and 'Castle' bogie, the water and coal capacities were as great as many a 4–4–0 tender engine of not so many years before. Frequently associated with and sometimes known as the 'Struan bankers', three or four were usually to be found at Blair Atholl, they were also employed on local passenger and trip workings around other parts of the system.

It is part of an engineer's duty before deciding on the final form of any design to investigate the feasibility of a fair range of possible solutions likely to suit the needs of his employers. In the case of Peter Drummond's work a number of preliminary general arrangement drawings have now come into the custody of the National Railway Museum at York and some details are listed in appendix 10. The first was entitled 'Sketch of improved 4 coupled passenger engine (Ben class)' and clearly represents an attempt to provide a longer boiler and firebox, but which was not pursued. The second 4–4–0 would seem more suited to a railway, where continuous fast running was possible, rather than hard uphill slogging even if relieved by some downhill sprints and may merely represent an attempt to see how the latest product of another works might look were it to appear from the Lochgorm stable. Although by no means large for its day the 0–4–4 tank of 1902 is still much bigger than the 'Passenger tank' actually produced three years later and it is interesting to note that the general arrangement drawing for the latter was also prepared in 1902. While the other 0–4–4T is simply a tank version of the 'Small Ben' and has a close affinity to the LSWR 0–4–4T 'M7' class. Perhaps most interesting are the two eight-coupled tender designs obviously for freight traffic. The mind boggles at such machines on the Highland line, where a wheel base of 19 feet would have been a severe handicap when it is realised that the 'Barney's' 16 ft 6 in was to its disadvantage. On the other hand they would have been a boon during the hard pressed times of World War I and as we know LMS Stanier 8F 2–8–0s with a 17 ft 3 in coupled wheel base eventually found their way up to Inverness during World War II.

The appearance of Peter Drummond's locomotive designs contrasted strongly with those of his predecessor David Jones and although lacking the grace they nonetheless had a workmanlike air. Except for the 'Castles' the two cylinders were now mounted between the frames with events regulated by Stephenson gear frequently actuated by a steam reverser, the safety valves were moved to on top of the dome in earlier designs but later reverted to the firebox, the cab front was squared off and fitted with round spectacles. The compensated suspension previously provided on all coupled engines was dropped and instead of the louvred double skin chimneys a built up design with cast iron rim was employed. The smokebox wing plates initiated with the 'Big Goods' and 'Lochs' were continued.

Students of locomotive design cannot help being struck by the likeness of Peter Drummond's engines to those of his elder brother Dugald. That there was close liaison between the two can hardly be denied, but that he went so far as to crib his brother's designs is unlikely. The relative dates of introduction of the various designs and features show that Dugald was the originator of the Drummond tradition and his standing amongst his contemporaries was high especially following his paper to the Institution of Civil Engineers in 1896. No doubt Peter believed that Dugald's ideas and layouts were good and used them himself as the occasion arose. He also took note of design changes instituted elsewhere, not least on his former company the Caledonian. Nevertheless the responsibility for adopting these features still rested with him and there is more to running a Locomotive Department than designing the motive power for its use. Although never attaining the heights of his brother he nonetheless moved on in February, 1912 to take charge of the locomotive affairs of the Glasgow and South Western Railway where he continued until his death in 1918.

FREDERICK G SMITH

To take Drummond's place his Assistant, Frederick George Smith, was promoted to Chief Mechanical Engineer. The first locomotives built during his tenure of office were a further batch of four 'Castles' to which a number of minor but not insignificant changes were made. These engines were supplied by the North British Locomotive Co. in 1913 and had longer smokeboxes than previous batches, some minor differences in the firebox proportions and solid 'big ends'. Whether the enlarged smokebox was intended to accommodate some form of superheater is not recorded, but it is known that Smith was experimenting with a Phoenix superheater on No. 141 ***Ballindalloch Castle*** at the time that this batch of 'Castles' was ordered.

Smith is of course best known as the locomotive engineer responsible for the ill-fated 'River' class of 4–6–0 locomotives. Conceived just before the on-set of World War I as an advancement on the previously mentioned 'Castle' class, by the time of their completion a year later the Highland Railway's Locomotive Department was nearing collapse due to the burden of handling the vast increase in traffic thrust upon it without prior warning following the outbreak of war. The arrival of these powerful engines should have greatly eased these problems, but on the delivery of Nos 70 and 71 the line's Chief Engineer prohibited the class on the ground that they were overweight and would therefore regularly overstress some under-bridges. Much as they were needed all six engines were sold to the Caledonian Railway at a small profit and Mr Smith forced to resign. In view of their subsequent return to the Highland Section of the LMS, following the strengthening and replacement of a few bridges and a better understanding of the loading imposed by locomotives in motion, the justification for these actions has been questioned. However, it may have been that it was Smith's handling of the Department as a whole and not least his allowing the back log of locomotive repairs to build up to such alarming proportions, which persuaded the Board to act as it did. Also it is one thing to undertake a programme of bridge renewals during peace time, but quite another in conditions of war, especially with the heavy load of vital war supplies and men passing along the line at the time.

It is said of Smith that he was unable to cooperate with other departmental heads and coordinate the work of his department with those of others. The incident of his placing an order with Cowans, Sheldon in 1913 for a new 60 foot diameter turntable for Inverness roundhouse, which subsequently had to be increased to 63 ft 4 in, is an example of his lack of liaison with the Engineer. Smith felt that, as the officer responsible for the turntable as a mechanism and the locomotives to be turned thereon, he should decide its diameter. Unfortunately he had overlooked the fact that the geometry of the permanent way with the closely radiating lines into each engine stall rendered the 60 foot diameter impossible. Close examination of the illustrations in this book will show that the first table and the 55 foot one installed circa 1883 were inside a series of rail crossings, whereas after 1914 the 'four foot' space between the rails of each radial line intersects its neighbour on both sides by all but the thickness of the two rail heads. The 60 foot diameter chosen by Smith fell within a zone where neither solution was practicable.

CHRISTOPHER CUMMING

The Highland Railway now reverted to a similar arrangement to that adopted by its early constituents, whereby the responsibility for locomotive design did not rest solely with an officer of the Company. If it had been in difficulties before, after the 'River' debacle its motive power position can only be described as desperate and swift action was taken by the Board. Even before Smith's departure arrangements had been initiated with the Railway Executive to borrow approximately twenty locomotives until such time as the HR's stock could be returned to full strength by overhaul or replacement, and for the next four years a motley collection of foreign engines was to be seen at work on the system. From the summer of 1915 plans were being developed for a superheated version of the 'Lochs' to handle the Northern Mail trains from Inverness to Wick and designs for these were completed by Hawthorn Leslie of Newcastle who built two, delivery being made in November, 1916. In addition during the interregnum before the appointment of C Cumming steps were taken to secure from the North British Locomotive Co. six more engines, three 4–4–0s of the 'Loch' class of D Jones' design dating back to 1896 complete with louvred chimneys and three 4–6–0 'Castles', however in the case of the latter a change was made to 6 foot diameter driving wheels and six wheeled tenders. It seems strange that 'Lochs' were chosen in lieu of further examples of the impending 'Snaigow' type, but it may have been that they were intended for the Kyle road upon which the 'Lochs' were the largest class permitted at the time. The three 'Castles' were no doubt an attempt to play it safe after the 'River' fiasco until such time as fresh designs could be worked up and approved, but the change of wheel diameter was probably more trouble than it was worth and this batch of engines was never as popular with enginemen.

Subsequently modernised versions of the 'Big Goods' and 'Castle' classes of 4–6–0 were designed and eight of each known respectively as the 'Superheated Goods' and 'Clans' were built, by Hawthorn Leslie between 1917 and 1921. As with the 'River' and 'Snaigow' types superheating, Belpaire fireboxes, Walschaerts valve gear, 10 inch diameter piston valves and larger cylinders were used to provide slightly more powerful locomotives than those they were intended to supersede. In view of the weight problem with the 'Rivers', the boilers and fireboxes were relatively small and their adhesive and total weights correspond very closely with those of their predecessors. Visually they were a marked departure from either Drummond or Jones designs and sported continuous splashers and roomy cabs with long projections of the roofs to the rear, although only the 'Clans' had the refinement of drum type smokeboxes and associated saddles.

The allocation of locomotives in the summer of 1919 is listed in appendix 11.

DAVID C URIE

Due to ill health Cumming was forced to retire shortly before grouping and for the last eight months of its separate existence locomotive affairs were in the charge of David Chalmers Urie, son of Richard W Urie the last Chief Mechanical Engineer of the London & South Western Railway. D C Urie had started his career on the LSWR under Dugald Drummond and came to the Highland after seven years with the Midland Great Western Railway of Ireland.

In the short time available the only work credited to him was the drawing up of plans to superheat the 'Big Bens', no doubt following the success his father achieved in applying superheat to D Drummond's saturated designs on the LSWR. The work was carried out during the early years of the LMS, but did not noticeably extend the life of these engines. With future knowledge of narrow piston valve rings and the retention of piston valves, the 'Lochs' might have been more suitable candidates for conversion.

D C Urie was one of several Highland Railway personalities to gain distinction on the railways following the amalgamation of 1923, soon becoming Mechanical Engineer for the Northern Division of the LMS at St Rollox responsible for all the Scottish lines and finally Chief of Motive Power for the entire railway in 1932. In the former post he was responsible for the fitting of standard Caledonian or Glasgow & South Western railways boilers to many Drummond and 'Loch' class locomotives, which while one may decry the sacrilege of defiling the Highland designs in such a manner, especially when later it led to the use of stove pipe chimneys, it undoubtedly resulted in longer working lives for the engines so treated.

The stock of locomotives taken over by the LMS at grouping is shown in appendix 2. Highland locomotives were held in high regard by the LMS authorities and initially this stud continued to work all the trains on the Highland Section as it was now termed. Examples of Midland 2–4–0 and 4–4–0 '2P' and 'Compound' classes, together with a LNWR 0–6–2T 'Coal Tank', were tried for short periods: while GSWR 2–6–0s designed by P Drummond, LMS Standard 4F 0–6–0, 3F 0–6–0Ts and later Stanier 2–6–2Ts were allocated for more permanent work. From the early 1930s various Caledonian classes including 4–4–0s of the 'Dunalastair' II, III and IV and Pickersgill designs, 0–6–0s of D Drummond 'Jumbo' and McIntosh '812' types, 0–4–4Ts again by D Drummond and McIntosh of the '439' class and 0–6–0T '782s' migrated north over the years, together with small four-coupled saddle tanks from the CR, L & Y and GSWR for use on the Harbour branch at Inverness, while GSW 0–6–2Ts went to Blair Atholl. Further details of allocations will be found in appendices 12 and 13.

Replacement of the top link classes started only in a small way in 1928-9 with the allocation of ten new 2–6–0 5P4F Horwich 'Crabs' Nos 13100 to 13109 for duties on the main line between Perth and Inverness. It was not until August 1934 that a significant change in the front line motive power occurred with the arrival of Stanier's famous 4–6–0 5P5F, some of the first of which found their way to Inverness, and as increasing numbers became available releasing all the 'Clans' and two 'Castles' for use on the Callender and Oban line and the gradual disappearance of the 'Crabs' to south of the Highlands. The process was only completed after World War II, when there were sufficient Stanier 'Black 5s' to work the Northern lines and the turntable at Kyle of Lochalsh was enlarged in 1946, thereby dispensing with the need for the continued existence of the 'Superheated Goods'. While the turntable at Kyle was out of commission 4P Fairburn designed 2–6–4Ts were used and this type subsequently found employ banking from Blair Atholl. The thirty remaining Highland locomotives to be nationalised on the setting up of British Railways at the beginning of 1948 are listed in appendix 3 and it was not long before these were to be withdrawn, the last a diminutive 0–4–4T No. 45 by then No. 55053 going rather suddenly in January, 1957 after breaking the crank axle.

In the following pages each class will be discussed in turn and their history traced, statistical and technical data being presented in tabular form in the appendices.

NUMBERING OF LOCOMOTIVES

As the Highland Railway's constituents acquired locomotives for the commencement of operations they numbered them in ascending order as a means of identifying the Company's assets. In the years that followed the cost of a new engine was either charged to the capital account, in which case it received the next number, or alternatively it was the replacement of existing stock and therefore took the previous engine's number, its cost being met by the revenue account. However, the displaced engine might still have some useful life left in it, albeit only on secondary duties, and would therefore have a suffix letter 'A' added to indicate that it was on the duplicate stock list. 'B' would be applied if the engine was returned to effective stock after the original number had already been taken by a new engine. The practice of numbering engines either to replace existing or as additions to the total stock meant that there was little consistency to the numbers of the new classes and, in an effort to give sequential numbers to some of these, it was not unusual for older engines to be renumbered several times before eventually finding their way onto the duplicate list, not that new engines were exempt from renumbering. In the lists of classes that follow, numbers allocated but not actually carried are shown in brackets.

The main purpose of the numbered stock list was to keep a record of the value of the Company's locomotives, even the cost of relatively minor improvements, such as the addition of steam heating cocks, sometimes being noted in the stock book. As appendix 14 shows in the days before rampant inflation the Company was able over the decades to go on replacing worn out locomotives at no appreciable increase in cost. For example one of Allan's early 2–4–0s acquired in 1858 for the sum of £2,776 was renewed forty one years later by provision of a 'Small Ben' for £2,493 10s 2d! This idyllic situation came to an end in 1919 when, as a result of rising material and labour costs during World War I, the 'Superheated Goods' and 'Clans' had to be bought at prices of £10,778 10s 4d and £9,152 18s 1d respectively, and in an effort to keep the books straight three or four older engines such as 'Clyde Bogies' and 'Straths' were temporarily at least placed in duplicate stock.

NAMING OF LOCOMOTIVES

The practice of naming locomotives originated early in the regime of the constituent companies and continued throughout the Highland Railway's existence, names being accorded to all passenger tender engines and some tank engines. The earliest single locomotives were called after some of the directors' country seats and were followed by the gentlemen's surnames which were applied to the 'Seafield' class, whilst the '18' and '36' classes took the names of towns and villages served by the newly opened railway. From an early date the habit of altering these names developed and in part may be due to the desire of the directors to be associated with the latest class of locomotive and not an outdated one relegated to secondary duties. To distinguish these, the names listed in the remainder of the book will where necessary be suffixed by a Roman numeral in brackets to indicate whether the engine referred to was the first or second etc. to carry that particular name. The numeral was of course not applied to the engine.

As already mentioned some tank engines were named and this was frequently done when the engine was allocated to work a branch line over a period and a name associated with the line was usually chosen. The problem arose when the engine was transferred elsewhere and this is another cause for the extensive renaming carried out by the Highland over the years.

The trend of naming locomotives after geographical locations was initiated with seven of the 'Duke' Class, which were given the title of some Highland counties and was extended by the 'Strath' class although actually it included as many glens. From the 'Lochs' onwards, with the exception of only *Snaigow* and *Durn*, all classes followed the chosen theme of bens, castles, rivers and clans, thereby conjuring up much of the romance of the Highland Railway. Despite the fact that these names were only painted on, the LMS and BR fortunately saw fit to continue the practice, thus bringing them to the attention of further generations.

TENDERS

The majority of Highland locomotives were equipped with tenders and the different types are listed in appendix 8, while the bunker and tank capacities of the tank engines are shown in appendix 9.

Although some designs of tender were coupled to more than one class, tender swopping was rife and few classes kept a single design throughout their lives.

The earliest locomotives were not equipped with brakes when built and until such time as these were added, reliance was placed on the screw brakes of the four and early six wheeled tenders. The Jones tenders of 2,100 and 2,250 gallon capacity were equipped with inside and outside bearings, thus making the wheels and axles interchangeable with the leading axle of the Allan locomotives. Coal rails were first fitted new to the 'Big Goods' and 'Loch' tenders and subsequently added to many older ones. The 'Loch' tenders were the first class to be equipped with footplate doors from the outset, a practice that was to continue on all future designs including tank engines, except the 'Rivers'. All Peter Drummond's tenders, save the 'Castles', were provided with wells thus making them suitable for the installation of his brother's patent feed water heaters, although this in fact was never carried out. Some tenders are known to have been provided with sieves to strain any solid matter that may have found its way into the water supply, which was in most instances taken direct from mountain streams. From about 1910 several tenders of 3,000 gallon capacity of both Jones and Drummond design together with at least one from a 'Strath' of 2,250 gallons, were enlarged by removing the tool box and extending the tank and coal rails.

LIVERIES

In considering the liveries carried by Highland locomotives it is as well to bear in mind that the period about to be briefly reviewed begins over 120 years ago, spans nearly seventy years and came under the jurisdiction of seven locomotive superintendents two of whom made radical changes during their tenure of office. Further, the application of his requirements was subject to interpretation by the paint shop foreman and the materials available to him.

Paintwork and Lining

Allan Those engines supplied under Allan's supervision were a dark green in colour picked out with numerous panels and boiler bands in broad black bands.

Stroudley It was on the newly formed Highland Railway that Stroudley first introduced his 'improved engine green', a colour that to most eyes appears as a dark yellow or golden ochre with perhaps a hint of green in certain lights. It is of course better known as 'Brighton yellow' to which railway he took it on his removal there in 1870. With the 'improved engine green' went a most elaborate scheme of lining out consisting of dark crimson bands with white and black lining. Smokeboxes, chimneys and tender axlebox horns were black and cab roofs white. The dark green livery continued to be applied to goods locomotives.

Figure 5

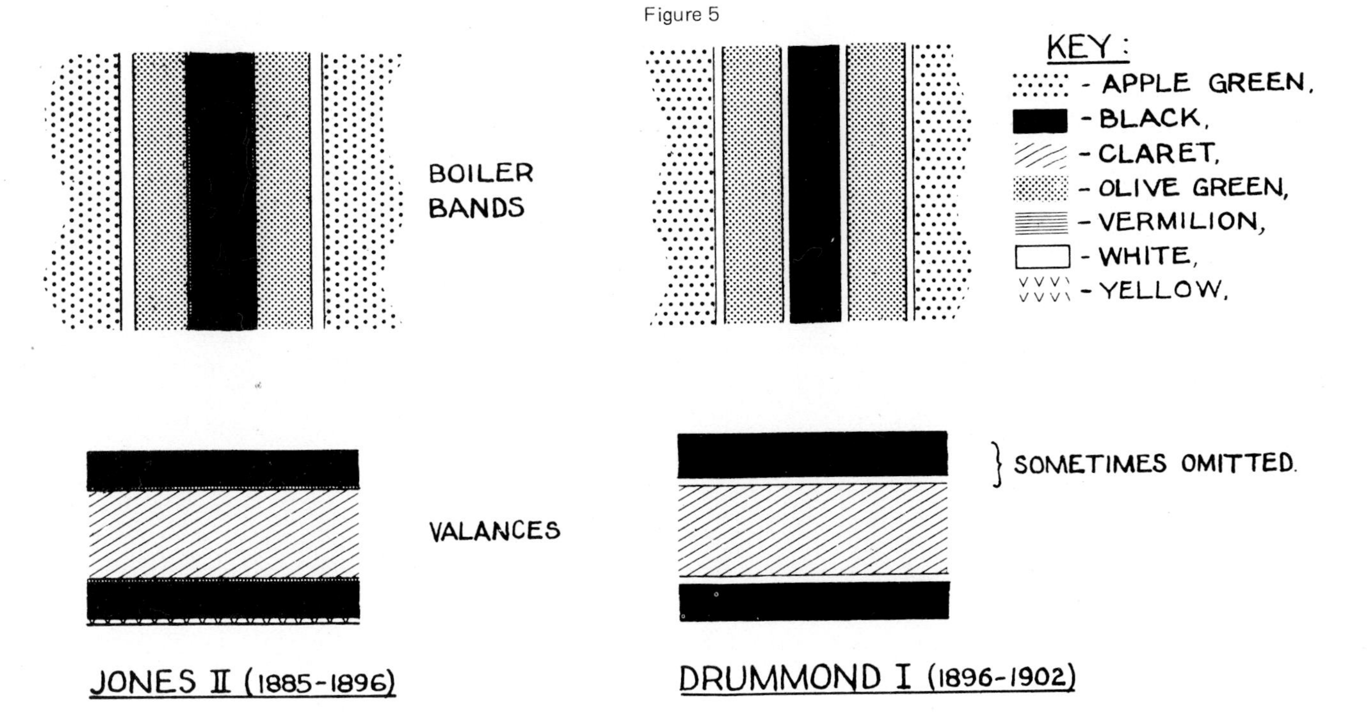

Jones I (1870-1884) During the early years of his office D Jones continued the Stroudley yellow livery for passenger engines and his new tank engines, but green with thin inner red and outer white lining. While from 1874 lined black was applied to goods engines. All types had vermilion buffer beams.

Jones II (1885-1896) From about 1885 both passenger and goods engines were painted in a new style of apple green with broad olive green bands edged with a thinner black band, itself lined white on the inside and vermilion outside. The boiler bands were black lined vermilion with olive green stripes each side lined outside with white on the boiler cladding. Both these arrangements are detailed in figure 5. Smokebox, footplate top, inner engine frame, tender top, axlebox horns and springs were all black. The cylinders were black also, but carried a large apple green panel lined white/black/vermilion. Claret was applied to the engine and tender footplate valances and steps, buffer housings and beam with a lined vermilion panel. The cab roof was again white and engine guard-irons vermilion.

Drummond I (1896-1902) For the first six years of P Drummond's period in command at Lochgorm an elaborate livery continued to be applied, indeed it was generally similar to the one previously in use except that the white and red lining was altered to a pair of white lines, see figure 5, and cab roofs were painted black instead of allowing time to make them so. Tender axle horns were changed to claret and all guard-irons black.

Drummond II (1902-1912) From the early years of this century the Highland Railway went through a further period of financial stringency resulting amongst other things in a change to an extremely austere locomotive livery. Gone were the claret, two tones of green and all vestige of lining. Instead one shade of dark olive green was applied to almost the whole engine and tender including the footplate valance, buffer beam and housings. As before the smokebox, chimney, footplate top, cab roof and tender top were black, and to these were added the tender frames.

Smith (1912-1915) This simple livery was perpetuated by Smith relieved only to the extent of a slight change in the green to a light moss colour and the restoration of vermilion buffer beams, snowplough angle irons and forward guard-irons. However, not many engines received this colour scheme due in part no doubt to the outbreak of World War I. During the war amongst other things several engines had their boilers painted black.

Figure 6

H . R

HIGHLAND RAILWAY.

THE HIGHLAND RAILWAY.

Plate 3

Figure 7

Cumming (1915-1922) Once again the shade of green was altered in general to a moss colour, but due to the difficulty during wartime of obtaining consistent stocks of paint and the fact that at the time many overhauls and repaints were being undertaken by outside works, the hue varied quite considerably. Reversing rods were painted green from this period and some coupling rods were also painted, probably red.

Urie (1922) Urie hardly had time to make much impact on the livery worn by Highland engines during the last few months of the Company's independent existence. However, it is recorded that a reversion to green buffer beams was carried out on one engine--No. 122 *Loch Moy*.

Polished metalwork

Up until grouping in 1923 many parts of the engines were brightly polished or burnished, as described below. Indeed the practice continued for some years after grouping, but gradually pride in appearance of the engines declined and nonferrous fittings were replaced by more mundane articles.

Brass	Safety valves, whistle, number plate, builders' plates, tender alarm bell and oil cups.
Burnished iron or steel	Handrails, grab irons, buffer heads, motion, reversing rods and couplings.
Copper	Lip of Allan, Stroudley and Jones chimneys and all exposed pipework.

Figure 8

To these embellishments must be added the unofficial adornments by enginemen, who, as the painted livery became less ornate, applied themselves to burnishing smokebox and wing plate front edges, hinges, darts and cylinder end covers and added such decorations as stars, shields, thistles and leaves to the smokebox doors.

Lettering

Company Title The company initials 'I. & A.J. Ry.' were painted in an arc around the leading splasher of 2–4–0 No. 11 in shaded serif lettering. The same style was adopted for 'No. 11' which was applied to the buffer beam.

During the whole of Jones' regime neither the Company's name nor initials were painted on any part of the engines or tenders. Drummond on the other hand applied the initials and number to the locomotive buffer beam both before and after the livery change in 1902, together with one of three possible styles of company initials or full title on the tender or tank sides, as shown in figure 6. There appears to be no logic as to why any particular example of the latter should have been chosen and most classes sported two types and several all three at one time or another. Smith and Cumming perpetuated the 'H.R', the second increasing the size from 9 by 7 inches to 12 by 9½ inches, although examples of the full company name and the Smith style of cab side numbers did occur. On the buffer beam Smith kept the initials and dropped the number, only to have Cumming reverse the procedure.

Names The earliest I & AJR engines were reported to have had small brass nameplates, but subsequently all names were painted in block style gilt letters with shading to the lower left in light green bordered in white and black. Letters were usually 4 inches high with the first sometimes of larger size. The names were formed round the leading splasher of all tender engines except the 4–6–0s. In the case of the 'Castles' the two words were written on the splasher in an arc over the first and second driving wheels, whilst the names of the 'Clans' were placed straight along the lower splasher. On tank engines the name was applied centrally across the tank and sometimes in a larger size.

Number plates

Stroudley introduced the elliptical brass number plate illustrated in plate 3 and figure 7. The edge and number were in relief and polished, whilst the Company's name and grooves were painted black and background to the numbers vermilion. This design lasted until on Drummond's arrival he altered it first to the style shown in figure 8 with the lettering and numbers in black and then in 1905 to the form depicted in plate 4 and figure 9. During World War I number plates were removed to provide brass for more essential fittings. Instead Smith fitted 5 inch numbers in bright metal to the smokebox doors and painted 9 inch numbers on the upper cab sides and the rear of tender or bunker. Cumming dropped the smokebox and cabside numbers reverting to the 1905 style of number plate, initially cast in gunmetal.

Builders' plates

Builders' plates followed each manufacturers' particular design and were usually cast in brass. Most were elliptical in shape with the notable exception of Dübs' diamond, which was taken up by the North British Locomotive Company. Early Hawthorn engines carried a squat cross shaped plate. Those for Lochgorm are shown in figures 10 and 11 and represent the styles used up to and following Drummond's arrival at Inverness. Lochgorm plates were also fitted to engines rebuilt there. All engines with Allan double framing had works plates fitted to the valance above the leading driving wheel. 'Lochs' and 'Castles' (I)s had theirs attached to the frames above the footplate, on both types of 'Ben' a place was found on the lower splasher over the leading driving wheel, whilst most other classes had theirs on the splashers until the Smith and

Plate 4

Figure 9

Figure 10

Figure 11

Cumming eras when the smokebox became the usual position. The rear and sides of the bunker were used for the 'Lochgorm' and 'Yankee' tanks respectively.

Coat of Arms

The coat of arms used by the Highland Railway consisted of the shields of the City of Perth and the Burgh of Inverness placed in front of an eagle and encircled by a light green garter with gold trimmings, bearing the inscription 'Highland Railway Company' in gold block letters shaded to the lower right. On the right hand side the shield of Inverness depicting Christ crucified marginally overlaps that of Perth, a lamb carrying St Andrew's flag. Both shields lean inwards and have red backgrounds with gold trimmings, all as illustrated in plate 2 on page viii.

Only a few first class passenger engines carried the coat of arms on the splasher in the last few years of the Company's existence. These included both ***Snaigow*** and ***Durn***, some 'Clans' and a few 'Castles'. The first two, however, had the garter alone when first built.

LMS Liveries

The livery of all LMS locomotives has been discussed in depth by R J Essery and D Jenkinson in their book ***Liveries of LMS Locomotives***, to which readers are referred. It is perhaps worth mentioning, however, some of the details peculiar to the ex Highland stock. The interpretation of passenger engine seems to have been fairly liberal resulting during the early years after grouping in a surprising number of classes privileged to wear the crimson lake livery. Whilst in no way wishing to belittle the Highland shades of locomotive green, if there had to be another colour, Derby's red could hardly have been more fitting. In the years following World War I Lochgorm had set about restoring the locomotive stock to first class working order and magnificent appearance and this superb finish continuing to be lavished on Highland engines in the years immediately following grouping.

With the change in style of LMS liveries in 1928 and drastic curtailment in the number of passenger locomotives eligible for the crimson lake colour scheme, in due course all remaining Highland locomotives appeared only in the black livery, although even so Lochgorm managed to apply red lining, strictly only for passenger engines, to a few goods engines. From the early '30s onwards the standard of finish and cleanliness deteriorated as the Highland's individuality became engulfed under the LMS corporate management. Examples are the misspelling of Gaelic names on engines repainted at southern works and the replacement of the Lochgorm builders' plates by the LMS standard article illustrated in plate 5.

The power classifications introduced by the LMS are listed in appendix 15 and the alterations instituted in 1928 should be noted. Prior to this date only passenger engines actually had the classification displayed on the upper cab side and the 'P' and 'F' was added from 1928 on. Initially the Highland Section seems to have placed quite a few of these in front of the power figure and examples of 'P2', 'P3' and 'P4' have been found amongst the 'Small Bens', 'Banking Tanks', 'Rivers', Nos 73 and 74 and the 'Clans'.

The few Highland engines to be given a repaint following nationalisation in 1948 all received British Railways' black livery with the addition of the red and grey lining to the last passenger tank engine by then No. 55053. The LMS power classification scheme was perpetuated by BR, without change in the case of the Highland stock.

Plate 5

2–2–2 'RAIGMORE' I CLASS

The first two locomotives of the 'Raigmore' class were delivered by sea to the Inverness and Nairn Railway and the others to the Inverness and Aberdeen Junction Railway. Up until 1858 they handled the entire goods and passenger traffic. All were built by Hawthorns of Leith and originally provided with weatherboards, but no cabs. Two safety valves were mounted on a domeless boiler as shown in figure 12 overleaf.

Figure 13 illustrates No. 1 *Raigmore* (I) as rebuilt by W Stroudley at Lochgorm in 1869 as a 2–4–0 with a cab for the enginemen. Whilst successful in improving the engine's performance the frames were found to be weak and when No. 2 *Aldourie* (I) was so treated new frames and a larger boiler were fitted, thus making it a virtually new engine, although a number of parts of the old No. 2 were reused. To make up the second pair of driving wheels, those from under Nos 3 and 4 were utilised and their boilers cut down for use on the 'Lochgorm' tanks.

Plates 6 and 7 are both of No. 2 following reconstruction at Lochgorm Works. Note the jack on the tender in plate 6 and that in the later view of No. 2 in plate 7 brakes had been added to the engine and two coal rails to the four wheeled tender whilst a smaller chimney cap has been fitted.

2–2–2 'RAIGMORE' (I) CLASS Total 4

No.	Works No.	Built	Name	With-drawn	Remarks
1	129	9/55	*Raigmore* (I)	'73	Rebuilt in '69 as 2–4–0
2	130	10/55	*Aldourie* (I)	2/71	Renewed in 2/71 as 2–4–0
3	146	8/56	*St Martin's* (I)	'69	
4	161	9/57	*Ardross* (I)	'70	

2–4–0 'No. 2' CLASS Total 1

No.	Built	Name	With-drawn	Remarks
2	2/71	*Aldourie* (II)	'03	Reused some parts from No. 2 ('55)

Renumbering:–

2 : 2A 5/98

Plate 6

Plate 7

2–2–2 'RAIGMORE' I CLASS

Figure 12

Figure 13

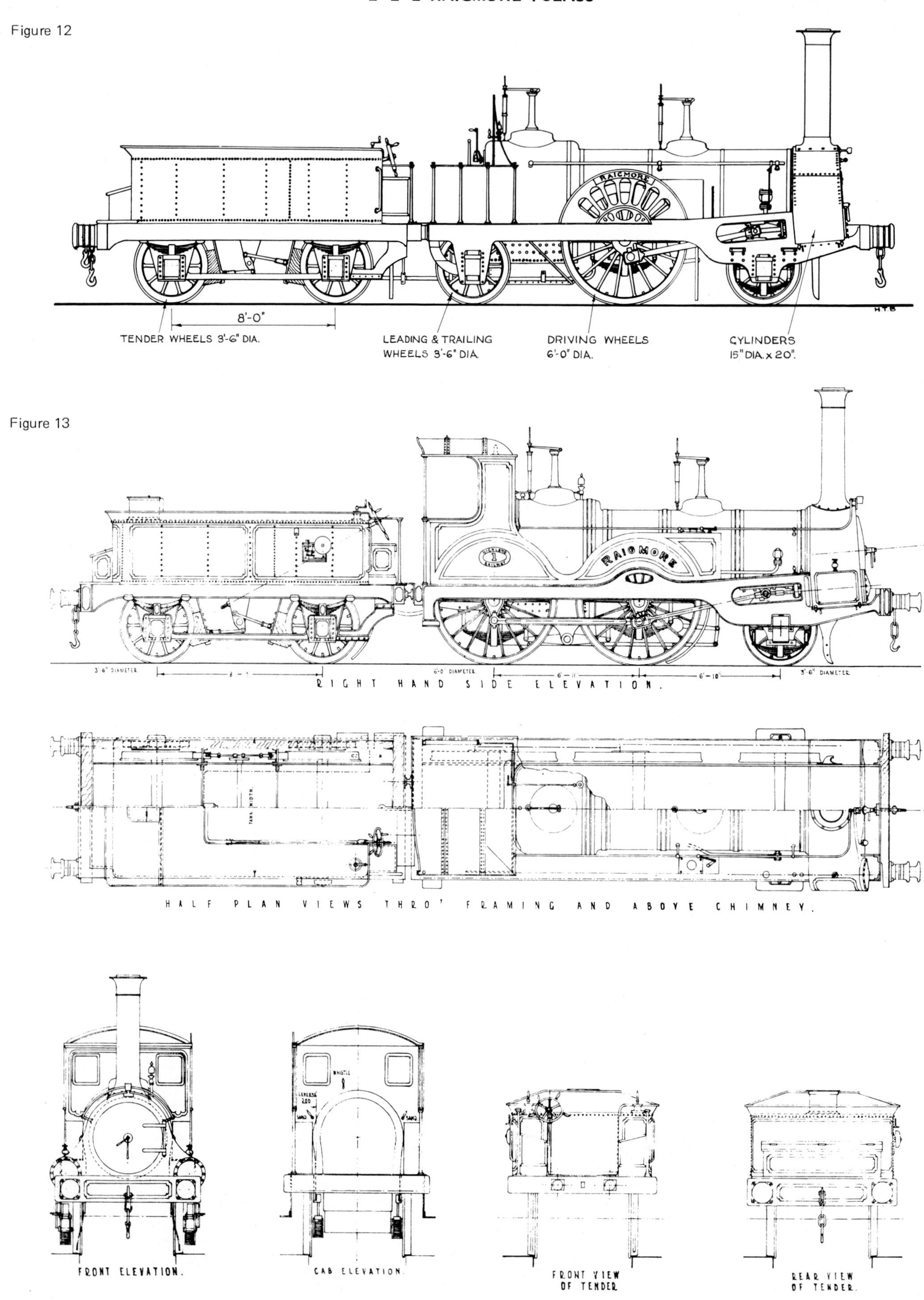

2–4–0 'SEAFIELD' CLASS

Plate 8

2–4–0 'SEAFIELD' CLASS Total 7

No.	Works No.	Built	Name	Rebuilt	Size of new cylinders, in.	With-drawn	Remarks
5	163	2/58	*Seafield* (I)	'80	16 x 24	5/97	
6	164	5/58	*Bruce* (I)	'74	16 x 23	'93	Sold 11/93
7	165	8/58	*Fife* (I)	5/75	17 x 24	5/99	
8	175	8/58	*Altyre*	2/86	16 x 24	5/93	
9	176	8/58	*Aultnaskiah* (I)	12/76	16 x 24		Sold 11/93
10	177	9/58	*Westhall*	6/73	17 x 24	5/97	
11	209	10/59	*Stafford* (I)	5/78	16 x 24	6/97	

These were the first engines to be designed especially for goods traffic on the I & AJR and plate 8 is of No. 11 in that company's livery. Panels in broad black lines can just be made out on the side sheets and tender, and the Hawthorn Works plate over the leading driving wheel on the outer side frame should be noted. Like the 'Raigmore' (I) class two safety valves were provided, but the one over the firebox passed through a dome. This distinction between passenger and goods types is a feature of all engines provided under Allan's supervision.

Over the years most engines were given standard chimneys and cabs, and had the cylinders increased in size as set out in the list adjacent, whilst Nos 7 and 10 were rebuilt as 4–4–0s and paired with six wheeled 1,800 gallon tenders, being the forerunners of the famous 'Skye Bogie' class. In plate 9 No. 7 is pictured following its withdrawal. No. 6 was lent to the Contractors in 1873 and worked for some time on the construction of the Sutherland & Caithness Railway.

Renaming:—

5 : —, *Tain.*
6 : —, *Helmsdale* (I) c '74.
7 : —, *Dingwall* (II) 5/75, — c '86.
8 : —, *Beauly* (II), —.
9 : —, *Golspie* (I), —.
10: —, *Duncraig* 6/73, —.
11: —, *Skibo,* —.

Renumbering:—

7 : 7A c '98.
11: 9 11/93.

Plate 9

2–2–2 'BELLADRUM' CLASS

Plate 10

Very similar in appearance to the 'Raigmore' (I) class, the 'Belladrum' class were provided with rather square cabs with square front windows and slightly larger cylinders. Ordered in the first instance for the opening of the Inverness and Ross-shire Railway, No. 12 ***Belladrum*** (I) is seen in plate 10 on the original timber decked turntable at Inverness roundhouse. The intricate lining out on every conceivable surface should be observed.

On completion of its rebuilding as a tank engine No. 12 worked on the Aberfeldy branch until 1879, for which purpose it was named ***Breadalbane*** (I). In 1885 it was again overhauled, fitted with a dome, put to work on the Strathpeffer branch and of course named ***Strathpeffer*** (I).

2–2–2 'BELLADRUM' CLASS Total 2

No.	Works No.	Built	Name	With-drawn	Remarks
12	258	5/62	*Belladrum* (I)	9/98	Rebuilt in 9/71 as 2–2–2T
13	259	7/62	*Lovat* (I)	5/1890	

Renaming:–

12: – c '64, ***Breadalbane*** (I) '71, – c '79, ***Strathpeffer*** (I) '85, – c '90.
13: *Thurso* '74.

Figure 14

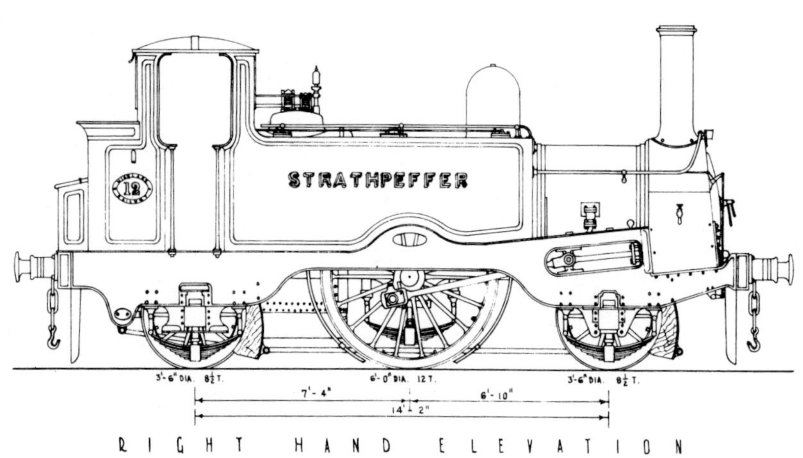

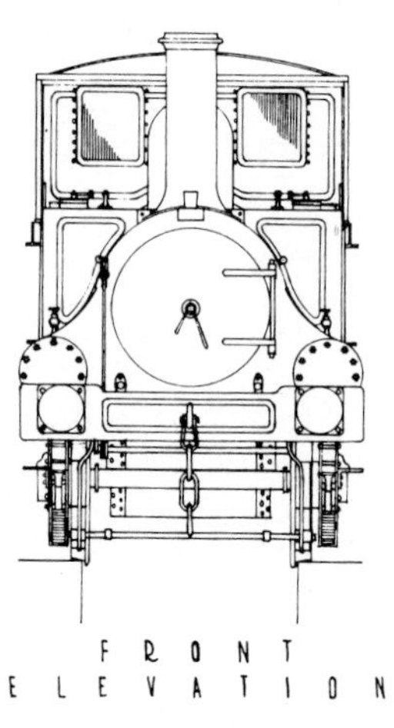

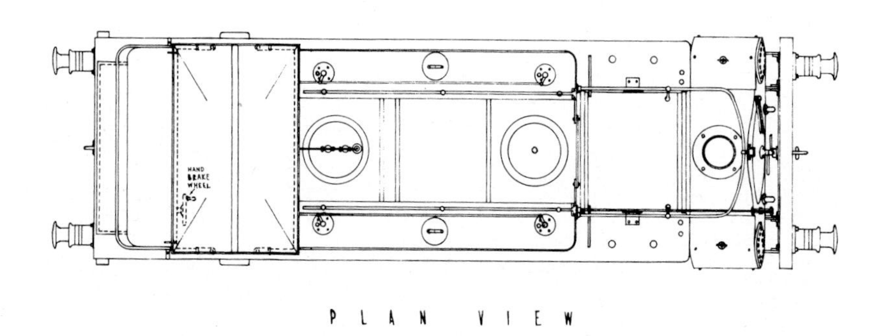

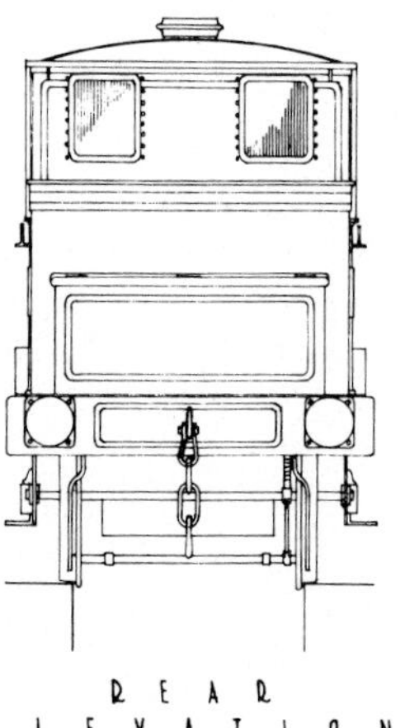

2–2–2T No. 12 and 2–4–0 '14' CLASS

Plate 11

Figure 14 shows No. 12 in its final form whilst plate 11 depicts the engine following its withdrawal from service.

Two goods engines were also added to stock in 1862 and again came from the Hawthorn stable. As supplied the fireboxes were of the Beattie type with a transverse midfeather and intended for coal burning. Rebuilding included enlarging cylinders to 17 by 24 inch and 5 ft 2½ in dia. driving wheels. In plate 12 ex No. 14 is portrayed as No. 6 following the first of its several renumberings. The Jones II livery scheme is clear on this view and also indicates that vacuum brake has been fitted.

2–4–0 '14' CLASS   Total 2

No.	Works No.	Built	Name	Rebuilt	With-drawn	Remarks
14	264	9/62	*Loch*	5/82	9/01	Sold 9/02
15	265	10/62	*Sutherland* (I)	9/86	'93	Sold 11/93

Renaming:–

14 : –, ***Evanton***, –.
15 : –, ***Dunkeld, Foulis,*** –.

Renumbering:–

14 : 6 11/93, 32 11/97, 49 2/99.

Plate 12

0–4–0T Nos. 16 and 17

No. 16 was originally built by Neilsons as a standard contractors box saddle tank and supplied to the Findhorn Railway in 1860. It passed to the I & AJR in April, 1862, and the indirect motion was replaced with Stephenson gear in 1866. Plate 13 depicts the engine after it had left railway service at work on a railway construction site, a duty more in line with its original conception.

Plate 13

FINDHORN RAILWAY 0–4–0 '16' CLASS Total 1

No.	Works No.	Built	Name	Withdrawn	Remarks
1	422	1859	*Findhorn*	9/72	Sold to H Mackenzie

Figure 15

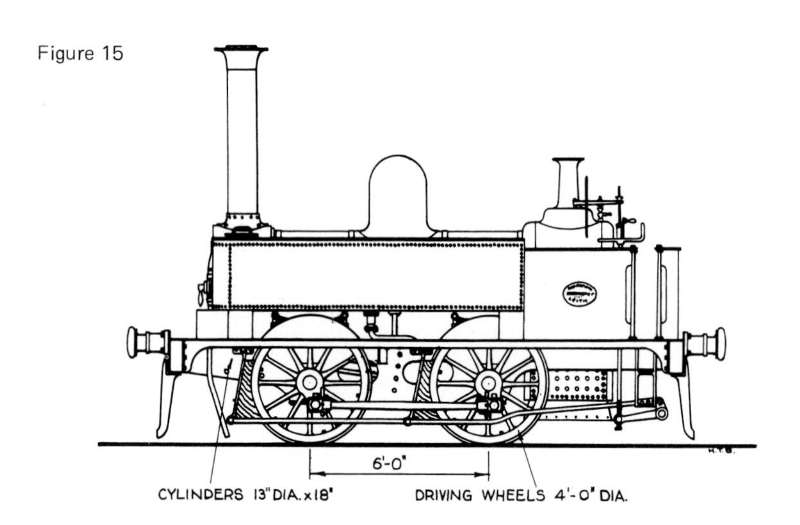

No. 17 on the other hand was built by Hawthorns for the I & AJR and was the first inside cylinder engine to be supplied to the railway. In the state shown in figure 15 it proved very unsteady while in motion and was in 1867 rebuilt as an 0–4–2T. For a number of years it was employed shunting in the Needlefield carriage works at Inverness. In 1886 it was converted to stationary use in the sawmill; only to be renovated in 1898, renumbered 1A, and resume shunting duties at the carriage works. After this somewhat chequered career it was eventually sold.

0–4–0T '17' CLASS Total 1

No.	Works No.	Built	Name	Rebuilt	Withdrawn
17	275	5/63	*Hopeman*	'67	'02

Renaming:

17 : –, ***Needlefield*** '80.

Renumbering

17 : 17A 12/79, – '80, 1A 9/83.

2–4–0 '18' CLASS

Plate 14

To handle the traffic on the new through route to the south over the Grampians, Allan put in hand the construction of a substantial number of new engines and placed an order with Sharp Stewart, then at Manchester, for ten goods engines of the '18' class. The boiler of No. 21 exploded in the vicinity of the firebox on 4th January, 1872 near Fochabers while working the 6.00 am Inverness to Keith goods train, and is clearly recorded by plate 14. Pieces of the engine were found up to 270 yards away. A brakesman who was riding on the footplate was killed and the fireman seriously injured, while the driver escaped with cuts and bruises. In this view the engine is generally in original condition and simple lining can be seen on the frames, cylinders, end of the buffer beam, step and cab side sheets.

2–4–0 '18' CLASS Total 10

No.	Works No.	Built	Name	Rebuilt with new cylinders 17 x 24	18 x 24	Withdrawn	Remarks
18	1416	8/63	*Inverness* (I)	1/72	8/87	'06	Sold 9/06.
19	1417	8/63	*Dingwall* (I)	11/71	8/79	'96	At Needlefield Sawmill until '03.
20	1426	8/63	*Birnam* (I)	6/72	2/82	'06	Sold 9/06.
21	1427	8/63	*Forres* (I)	4/74	4/84	7/09	Sold 9/09.
22	1436	9/63	*Aviemore* (I)	3/73	8/78	'96	
23	1437	10/63	*Murthly*	9/73	2/91	'02	Sold 9/02.
24	1438	10/63	*Invergordon* (I)	—	9/76	'04	
25	1439	10/63	*Novar*	—	2/90	'05	
26	1440	11/63	*Beauly* (I)	—	8/93	'96	Written off 7/03.
27	1441	11/63	*Conon*	—	2/91	'23	

Renaming:—

19 : —, *Golspie* (II), — c '86.
23 : —, *Dalcross*, —.
24 : —, *Lairg.*
All except No. 24 lost their names prior to their withdrawal.

Renumbering:—

18 : 36 8/02.
20 : 38 8/02.
21 : 39 8/02.
27 : 27A '13, 27B '16, 27A 4/18.

2–4–0 '18' CLASS

Plate 15

Over the years the engines were rebuilt with larger cylinders, wheels and fitted with Jones' design of boiler and cab, together with numerous standard fittings including louvred chimney, lubricators and engine brakes. Figure 16 is a drawing of the engine as built, whilst plate 15 illustrates No. 20 in its final form and another view of the rebuilt version will be found as the frontispiece of No. 27A standing outside Perth engine shed in the Drummond II livery. This engine went on to reach the grouping, but was withdrawn without receiving an LMS number.

Figure 16

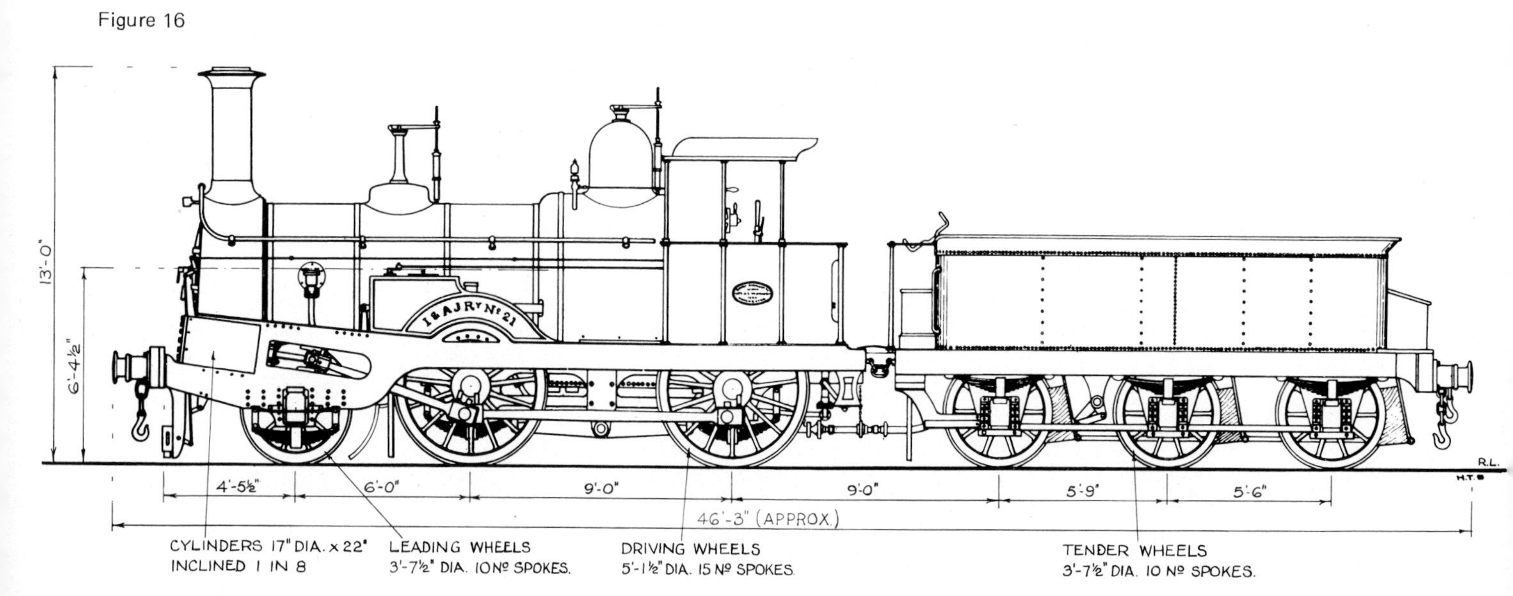

2–2–2 'GLENBARRY' CLASS

Plate 16

For passenger traffic eighteen 2–2–2s were put in hand, all but the first two being completed by Neilsons in two batches. The two odd men out were the last locomotives supplied by Hawthorns of Leith to the I & AJR and cost considerably more than the others. Apart from generally increased dimensions the 'Glenbarries' were very similar to the previous two passenger classes. Plate 16 shows No. 35 in workshop grey and without a tender. Note the snow brushes mounted on the front guard-irons and the steam pipes behind the leading wheels intended to blow away snow.

As built Nos 28 to 35 had a longitudinal mid-feather in the firebox and two doors, and Nos 46 to 54 had Beattie fireboxes, whilst last but by no means least No. 55 had a plain firebox.

2–2–2 'GLENBARRY' CLASS Total 18

No.	Builder	Works No.	Built	Name	Renamed	Date	Rebuilt as 2–4–0	18"x24" cyl.	new boiler	Withdrawn	Remarks
28	Hawthorns	299	9/63	*Glenbarry*	*Grantown*	5/96	8/72	8/72	2/96	'98	Written off 7/03
29	Hawthorns	300	10/63	*Highlander* (I)	*Forres* (II)	5/79	8/71	8/71	5/96	'98	
30	Neilson	966	10/63	*Prince*	–	–	9/91	u/k	9/91	'93	
31	Neilson	967	10/63	*Princess*	–	–	5/84	u/k	'95	2/98	Sold '99
32	Neilson	968	10/63	*Sutherland* (II)	*Cluny* (II)	'74	–	2/89	–	9/98	
33	Neilson	969	10/63	*Atholl* (I)	*Birnam* (II)	8/86	3/83	u/k	–	'98	
34	Neilson	970	10/63	*Seafield* (I)	*Perthshire* (II)	c '89	12/83	u/k	9/93	4/97	
35	Neilson	971	11/63	*Kingsmills*	*Isla Bank*	c '88	7/92	u/k	7/92	8/23	
46	Neilson	1055	6/64	*Clachnacuddin* (I)	*Kingussie* (II)	'83	8/80	2/96	2/96	'06	
47	Neilson	1057	6/64	*Bruce* (II)	*Lovat* (II)		6/80	8/95	8/95	'06	
48	Neilson	1056	6/64	*Cadboll* (I)	*Dingwall* (III)	'86	1/81	1/81	–	9/92	
49	Neilson	1058	7/64	*Belladrum* (II)	*Helmsdale* (II)		4/79	u/k	'94	7/99	Sold '99
50	Neilson	1059	7/64	*Aultnaskiah* (II)	*Badenoch*		4/78	–	–	4/97	
51	Neilson	1054	5/64	*Caithness* (I)	*Blair-Atholl*	'74	7/75	–	u/k	'93	
52	Neilson	1060	9/64	*Dunphail*	–	–	2/76	–	–	'99	
53	Neilson	1061	9/64	*Stafford* (II)	*Golspie* (III)	'86	11/73	–	–	'93	
54	Neilson	1062	10/64	*Macduff*	–	–	8/73	–	–	'98	Sold 11/03
55	Neilson	1063	10/64	*Cluny* (I)	*Sutherland* (III)	'74	9/74	–	1/95	'06	Sold '06

Additional Renaming:–

29: – c '98.
47: *Beauly* (III) '86.
55: *Invergordon* (II) '84.

Renumbering:–

35: 35A 2/11.

2–2–2 'GLENBARRY' CLASS

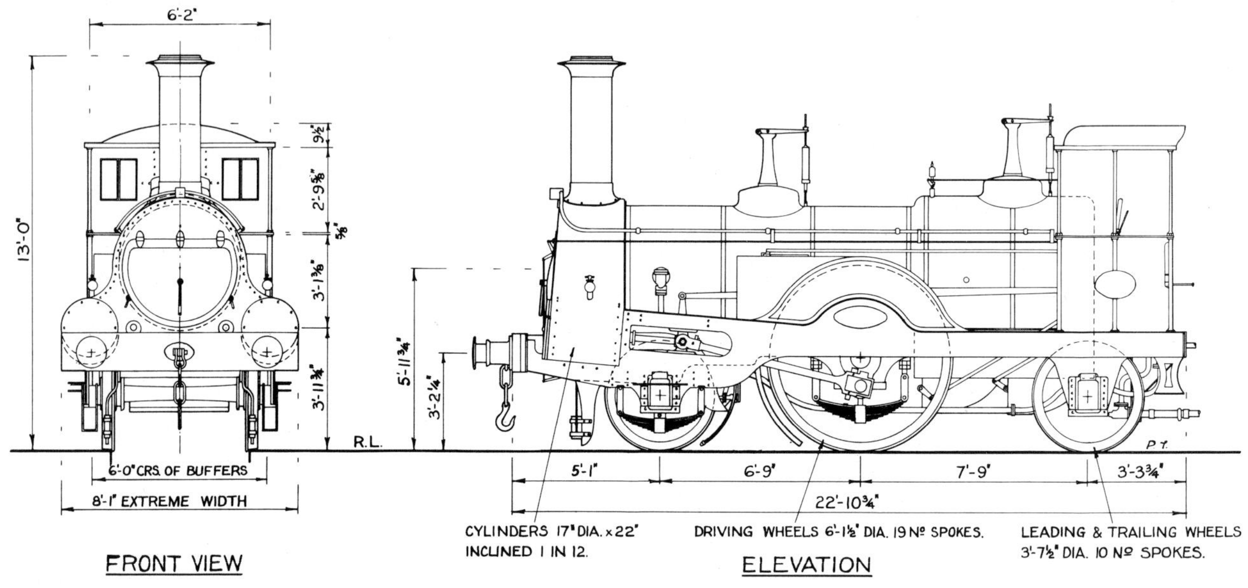

Figure 17

Figure 17 is of the 'Glenbarry' class as built, the tender being to the same design as the '18' class for which there is a drawing on the previous page. All except No. 32, shown in plate 18 late in life when named ***Cluny*** (II), were rebuilt as 2–4–0s many with cylinders enlarged to 18 by 24 inches. Ten of the class were reboilered and provided with 6 ft 3 in driving wheels between 1881 and 1896.

Plate 17

In plate 17 No. 29 ***Forres*** (II) is seen at Inverness rebuilt as a 2–4–0, but with an original boiler. Unusually it has a cab with square corners.

Plate 18

2–4–0 REBUILT 'GLENBARRY' CLASS

Plate 19

Plate 19 is of No. 50 ***Badenoch*** also as a 2–4–0 and original boiler but more common round cornered cab. No. 35 distinguished itself by reaching the LMS lists, not, however, receiving an LMS number and plate 20 shows her as No. 35A ***Isla Bank*** at Aviemore on 27th August 1923. The Drummond I ornate livery is very apparent on No. 55 ***Invergordon*** in plate 21.

Plate 20

Plate 21

2–4–0 '36' CLASS

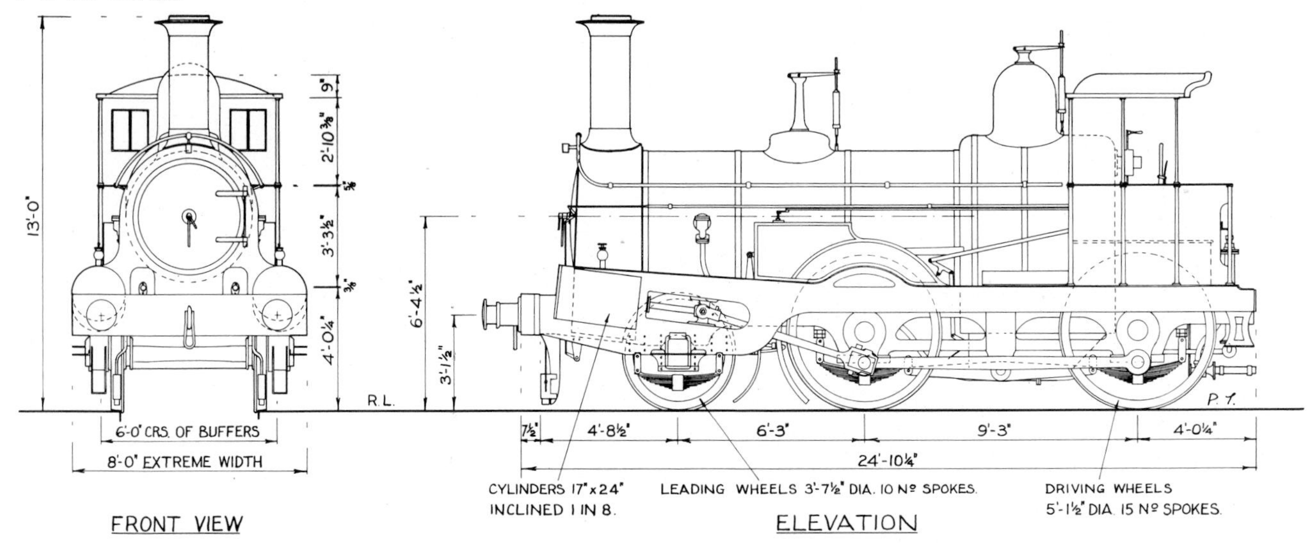

Figure 18

2–4–0 '36' CLASS Total 10

No.	Works No.	Built	Name	Rebuilt	With-drawn	Remarks
36	1506	4/64	*Nairn*	7/76	'02	Sold 9/02.
37	1507	4/64	*Struan*	2/86	'15	Sold 10/15.
38	1508	4/64	*Kincraig*	8/82	'02	Sold 9/02.
39	1509	5/64	*Aviemore* (II)	8/84	'02	Sold '02.
40	1510	5/64	*Keith*	8/85	'05	
41	1511	5/64	*Kingussie* (I)	8/87	'06	
42	1512	5/64	*Lentran*	2/83	'23	
43	1513	6/64	*Dava*	8/80	'98	Written off 7/03.
44	1519	6/64	*Brodie*	2/79	'12	Sold 7/12.
45	1520	6/64	*Dalcross*	2/89	'05	

Renaming:—

All engines eventually lost their names.

Renumbering:—

41: 41A '05.
42: 42A 1/12, 37 10/15, 37A 4/18.
44: 44A 2/12.

The '36' class were almost identical with the '18' class except for an increased wheel base, larger boiler, cylinders and fireboxes which were of the Beattie type when built by Sharp Stewart. These engines were also I & AJR goods locomotives and the last class associated with Alexander Allan. All were rebuilt between 1876 and 1889 with 18 by 24 inch cylinders, 5 ft 3 in driving wheels and 3 ft 9 in leading and tender wheels, together with numerous standard fittings. No. 37, although sometimes quoted as passing to the LMS in 1923 was in fact withdrawn in 1915. It was the original No. 42, becoming No. 37 in 1915, in common with two other 2–4–0s, which actually achieved this distinction. None of them ever received LMS numbers.

Figure 18 is a drawing of the class as built, the tender being to the same design as the '18' class and plate 22 depicts No. 38 in its final form.

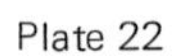

Plate 22

0–6–0ST 'LOCHGORM TANK' CLASS

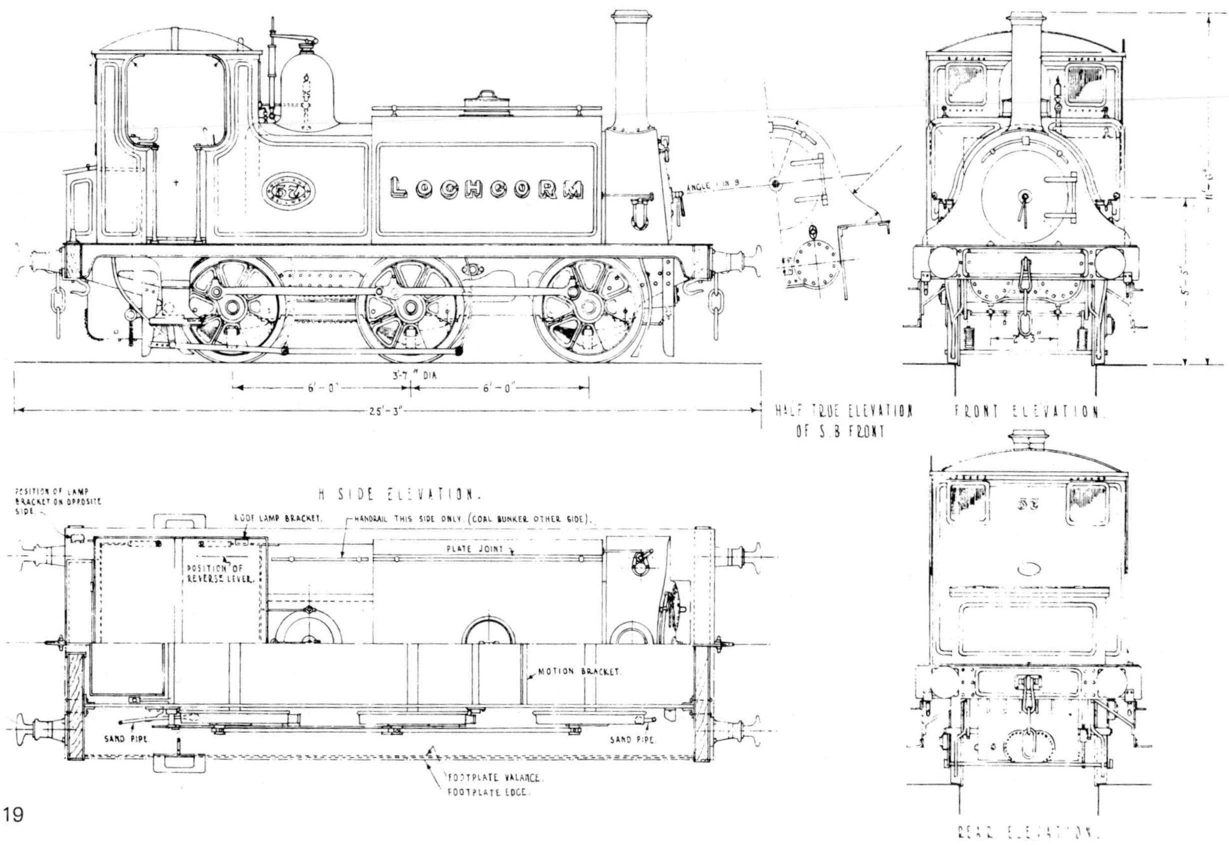

Figure 19

These saddletanks represent the only fresh design introduced to the Highland Railway by Stroudley, but are of historic interest as being the prototype for the famous Stroudley 'Terriers' of the London Brighton & South Coast Railway. They were also the first engines to be built at the Highland Company's Lochgorm Works at Inverness. The original boilers fitted to this class were not new, being those recovered from three of the 'Raigmore' I class. They were reboilered in 1896 and '97.

0–6–0ST 'LOCHGORM TANK' CLASS — Total 3

HR No.	Built	Name	Rebuilt	LMS No.	Withdrawn
56	4/69	*Balnain*	2/96	16118	12/27
57	11/72	*Lochgorm*	8/97	16119	12/32
16	10/74	*St Martin's* (II)	6/96	16383	1/27

Renaming:–

56 : *Dornoch* '02.
16 : *Fort George* '99

Renumbering:–

56 : 56A 7/19, 56 9/19, 56A 7/21, 56B 5/22.
57 : 57A 7/21, 57B 5/22.
16 : 49 2/01, 49A 7/12.

Figure 19 is of No. 57 *Lochgorm* in as built condition, while plate 23 shows the same engine after grouping although still in Highland livery. Note the revised chimney, safety valve and coal bunker added on the rear.

Plate 23

Plate 24

Plate 25

As these three photographs demonstrate all three engines of this class passed into the LMS and were painted in a couple of variations of that company's black livery. In plate 24 former No. 57 is seen on the turntable at Inverness as LMS No. 16119 and the power classification '2F' may be discerned on the upper front cab sheet. It is nonetheless lined in red, a feature intended for mixed traffic engines.

No. 56 was rebuilt with extended side tanks and plate 25 illustrates this engine later in life, again on the Inverness turntable and numbered LMS 16118. For some obscure reason No. 16 was given an LMS number following on the three Drummond 0–6–0T 'Scrap Tanks', yet to be described, and plate 26 shows it standing at Inverness. This and the previous engine are in the earlier LMS goods engine livery with the company's initials in a vermilion panel on the cab side. Different pattern wheels can be seen on all three engines.

Plate 26

Plate 27

To replace Allan's passenger engines on principal express trains Jones' first new design was the bogie four coupled 'Duke' class built by Dübs of Glasgow in 1874. At the time of their introduction they were the most powerful engines in the country and they must have made previous Highland engines appear insignificant in comparison. Originally fitted with Le Chateliers' counter pressure brake, vacuum brake was subsequently added under the cab in place of a small cast iron feed tank. Westinghouse brake was also fitted to Nos 62 and 64 for a period. Although the 1,800 gallon six wheeled tender was continued, it was to a new design with an outside frame enclosing the springs. In later years these tenders were frequently exchanged for those of the 'Skye Bogie' class. The boiler was made up in three rings with the dome mounted on the middle ring. Two Adams' column type safety valves were placed transversely on the firebox and this was the first new design to mount the famous louvred chimney.

Plate 27 illustrates No. 61 ***Duke*** in Jones II livery whilst plate 28 is of No. 68 ***Muirtown*** newly out of the paint shop in the earlier Drummond style of lining and with the lubricators repositioned on the smokebox front. A drawing in figure 20 and the class list is reproduced overleaf.

Plate 28

4–4–0 'DUKE' CLASS

Figure 20

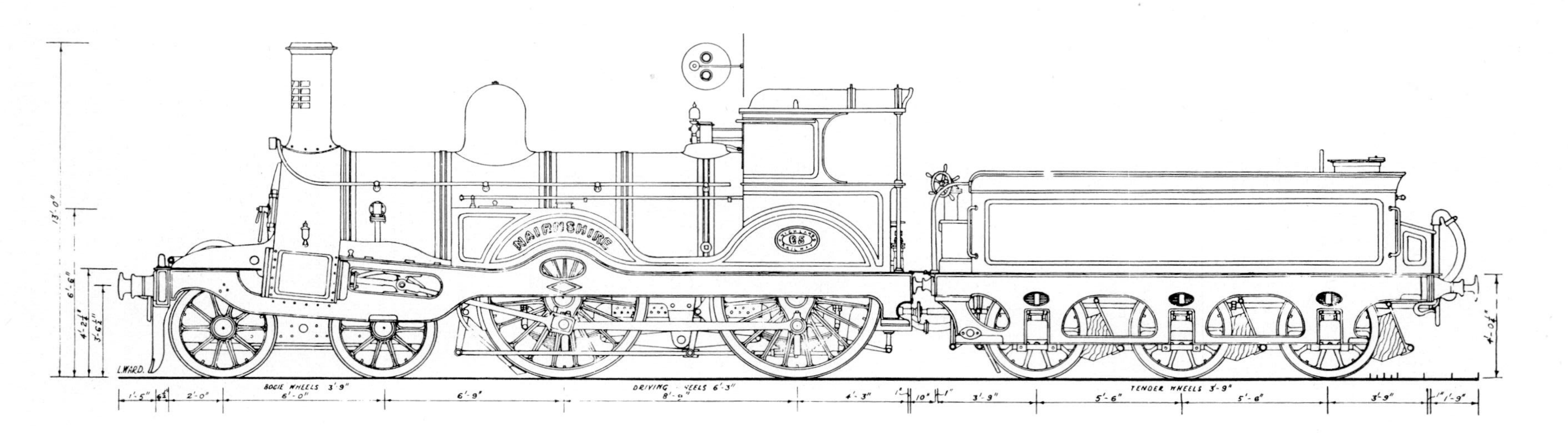

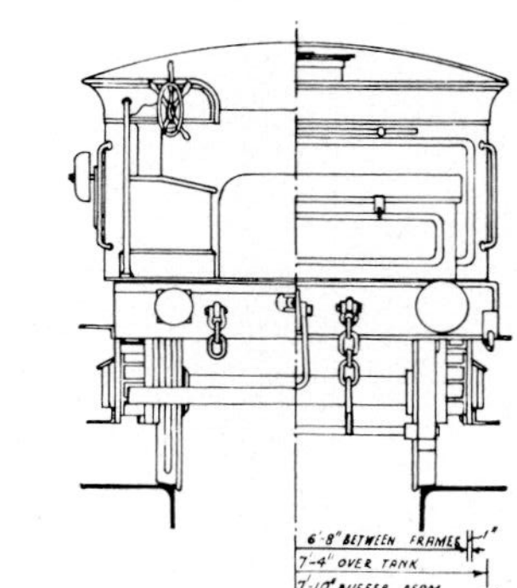

4–4–0 'DUKE' CLASS Total 10

No.	Works No.	Built	Name	Renamed	Date	Rebuilt		With-drawn	Sold
60	714	6/74	*Bruce* (III)	*Sutherland* (IV)	6/84	2/88	8/98	8/08	9/09
61	715	6/74	*Sutherlandshire*	*Duke*	1/77	8/89	12/98	'07	8/07
62	716	6/74	*Perthshire* (I)	*Stemster*	'89	2/87	5/99	8/08	9/09
63	717	7/74	*Inverness-shire*	*Inverness* (II)		8/87		'07	8/07
64	718	7/74	*Morayshire*	*Seafield* (III)	c.'89	2/88		9/09	
65	719	7/74	*Nairnshire*	*Dalraddy*		2/88		1/09	9/09
66	720	7/74	*Ross-shire*	*Ardvuela*		8/88	4/00	'07	8/07
67	721	8/74	*The Duke*	*Cromartie*	1/77	8/89	2/98	'23	
68	722	8/74	*Caithness-shire*	*Caithness* (II)		2/88	9/98	'07	8/07
69	723	8/74	*The Lord Provost*	*Sir James*		8/88	8/98	1/09	9/09

Additional renaming:—

62 : ***Huntingtower*** '99, ***Aultwharrie*** '03.
68 : ***Muirtown.***
69 : ***Aldourie*** (III) c.'03.

Renumbering:—

67 : 70A 2/23.

Plate 29

4–4–0 'LOCHGORM BOGIE' CLASS Total 7

No.	Built	Name	Withdrawn	Remarks
4	7/76	*Ardross* (II)	'13	Sold 3/13.
71	12/83	*Clachnacuddin* (II)	'15	Sold 10/15.
72	7/84	*Bruce* (IV)	'23	Sold 12/23.
73	1/85	*Thurlow*	'23	
74	9/85	*Beaufort*	2/15	Tender broken up 7/22.
75	10/86	*Breadalbane* (III)	8/23	
84	12/88	*Dochfour*	'23	

Renaming:–

4 : *Auchtertyre* '01
72 : *Grange* '86
73 : –, *Rosehaugh* '98

Renumbering:–

4 : 31 2/99, 31A 9/11.
71 : 71A 7/12.
72 : 72A 7/13.
73 : 73A 12/16.
75 : 75A 3/17.
84 : 84A 4/17.

Plate 30

Two years after the delivery of the 'Duke' class, Lochgorm put in hand the construction of a similar engine and between 1883 and '88 built six more, the latter having subtle differences such as longer buffers, a shorter boiler pressed to 150 instead of 140 lb/sq in pressure, and 2,250 gallon tenders with the springs mounted outside the frames and the same as the tender drawn in figure 23. Nos 71 and 72 were for a while provided with Westinghouse brake gear for the working of through trains from neighbouring companies.

Plates 29 and 30 show No. 4 ***Ardross*** (II) and No. 72 ***Grange*** both in Drummond I livery. Notice the different tenders and the alarm bell and Westinghouse pump on No. 72.

Plate 31

Plate 31 illustrates No. 75 ***Breadalbane*** (III) at Inverness later in life wearing the plain unlined livery and yet, apart from minor details such as the addition of tender doors and coal rails, the engine is almost in original condition. Note the folded vacuum brake pipe in front of the smokebox door.

To replace two of the rebuilt 'Raigmore' (I) class for use on secondary duties, Lochgorm constructed two new 2–4–0s with what were to become the later standard replacement components for the Allan engines, although the cylinder diameter was smaller than usual.

2–4–0 'RAIGMORE' (II) CLASS Total 2

No.	Built	Name	Withdrawn	Remarks
3	7/77	*Ballindalloch*	'12	Sold 7/12
1	9/79	*Raigmore* (II)	'10	

Renumbering:—

3 : 30 3/98
1 : 29 5/98, 29A 8/10.

Plate 32 is interesting because it is of No. 1 ***Raigmore*** (II) as built in 1877 and the lining to the driving wheel compensation beam and fulcrum is an indication of the extreme lengths to which embellishments were taken in those far off days.

Plate 32

2–4–0T 'JONES TANK' CLASS

2–4–0T 'JONES TANK' Total 3

HR No.	Built	Name	Rebuilt as 4–4–0T	LMS No.	Withdrawn
58	12/78	***Burghead***	'85	15011	2/28
59	6/79	***Highlander*** (II)	6/87	15010	11/32
17	12/79	***Breadalbane*** (II)	7/87	15012	11/29

To supplement Stroudley's 0–6–0T 'Lochgorm Tanks' Jones built at Lochgorm three somewhat larger 2–4–0 tank engines. As well as carrying out shunting duties, these were tried on the Aberfeldy and Burghead branches, but on this work their rigid wheelbase was found to be an embarrassment and, like Nos 7 and 10 of the 'Seafield' class, they were within eight years rebuilt with a leading bogie, in which form they lasted for many years. Drawings of both arrangements will be found in figure 21.

Renaming:–

17: *Aberfeldy* '86, – '06.
58 and 59 had their names removed in 1900.

Renumbering:–

58: 58A 12/12, 58B 8/22.
59: 59A 12/12, 59B 8/22.
17: 50 11/00, 50A 12/12, 50B 8/22.

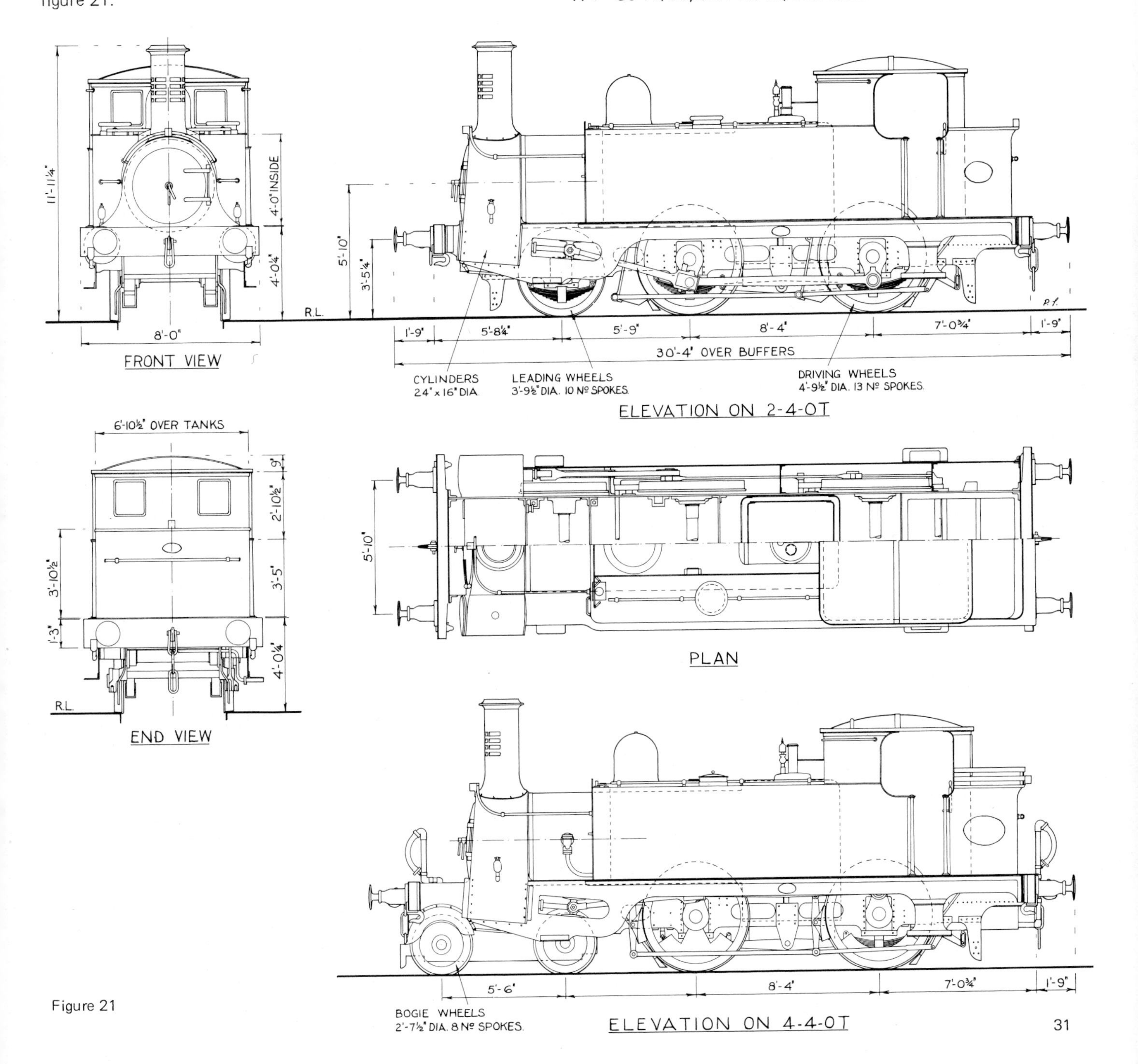

Figure 21

4–4–0T 'JONES TANK' CLASS

Plate 33

Fresh from the paint shop No. 58B is seen in plate 33 in rebuilt form on the Inverness turntable on rather a dull day. Note that the 'B' suffix to the number is painted above the number-plate, coal rails have been added to the bunker, a Drummond cap fitted to the chimney and vacuum brake provided. The boiler and firebox on this engine is reputed to have remained unchanged throughout the life of the engine.

Plates 34 and 35 show No. 50B at Perth in both cases where the engine was a familiar sight as station pilot. This engine was fitted by Drummond with a larger boiler as seen in the photographs. Steam heating hoses are also apparent at both front and rear.

Plate 34

Plate 35

Plate 36

All three engines passed into LMS ownership, received numbers and the crimson lake livery accorded to all passenger classes for the first five years and plate 36 illustrates the style on No. 15012 with the larger boiler at Perth in May 1928.

No. 59 as 15010 survived long enough to be repainted in the black livery with rearranged company initials and number, as depicted in plate 37 of this engine at Inverness in 1930.

Plate 37

Plate 38

After the 4–6–0 'Big Goods', yet to be described, the 'Skye Bogie' class must be the best known of Jones' designs. As its name implies, the class was primarily intended to work the Dingwall and Skye line and was the result of earlier experiments with the 2–4–0s Nos 7 and 10 rebuilt as 4–4–0s. Figure 22 shows goods engine wheels of 5 ft 3 in dia. fitted to frames and boiler based closely on his earlier highly successful 'Duke' class of 4–4–0 passenger engines.

For the first ten years of its life No. 70 must have shared workings on the Skye line with Nos 7 and 10, and it was only with the impending extension from Strome Ferry to Kyle in 1893 that further engines were added to the 'Skye Bogie' class.

In plate 38 the first engine No. 70 is seen resplendent in Drummond's earlier livery with full lining and a tender, as yet without coal rails, while in plate 39 No. 86 outside Kyle shed is in plain livery and 'H.R 86' on the front buffer beam, but nothing apparent on the tender side.

Plate 39

Figure 22

4–4–0 'SKYE BOGIE' CLASS

1'-6" DIA.
4'-0"
2'-3" DIA.
6'-3"
3'-4¾"
1'-9" | 2'-3½" | 6'-0" | 6'-9" | 8'-9" | 4'-4" | 4'-11" | 6'-0" | 6'-0" | 5'-9½"
52'-7" OVER BUFFERS
BOGIE WHEELS 3'-3" DIA. 8 Nº SPOKES.
CYLINDERS 18" DIA. x 24" INCLINED 1 IN 12.
DRIVING WHEELS 5'-3" DIA. 15 Nº SPOKES.
TENDER WHEELS 3'-9" DIA. 10 Nº SPOKES.
P. Y.

ELEVATION

8'-3" EXTREME WIDTH
7'-1" OVER FOOTPLATE
5'-10" BUFFER CRS.

PLAN

6'-5" OVER CAB
9½"
2'-10½"
3'-5"
3'-11"
R.L.

FRONT OF ENGINE

FRONT
REAR
OUTER FRAME

DEVELOPED SHAPE OF HALF SMOKEBOX/CYLINDER WRAPPER

FRONT OF TENDER

REAR OF TENDER

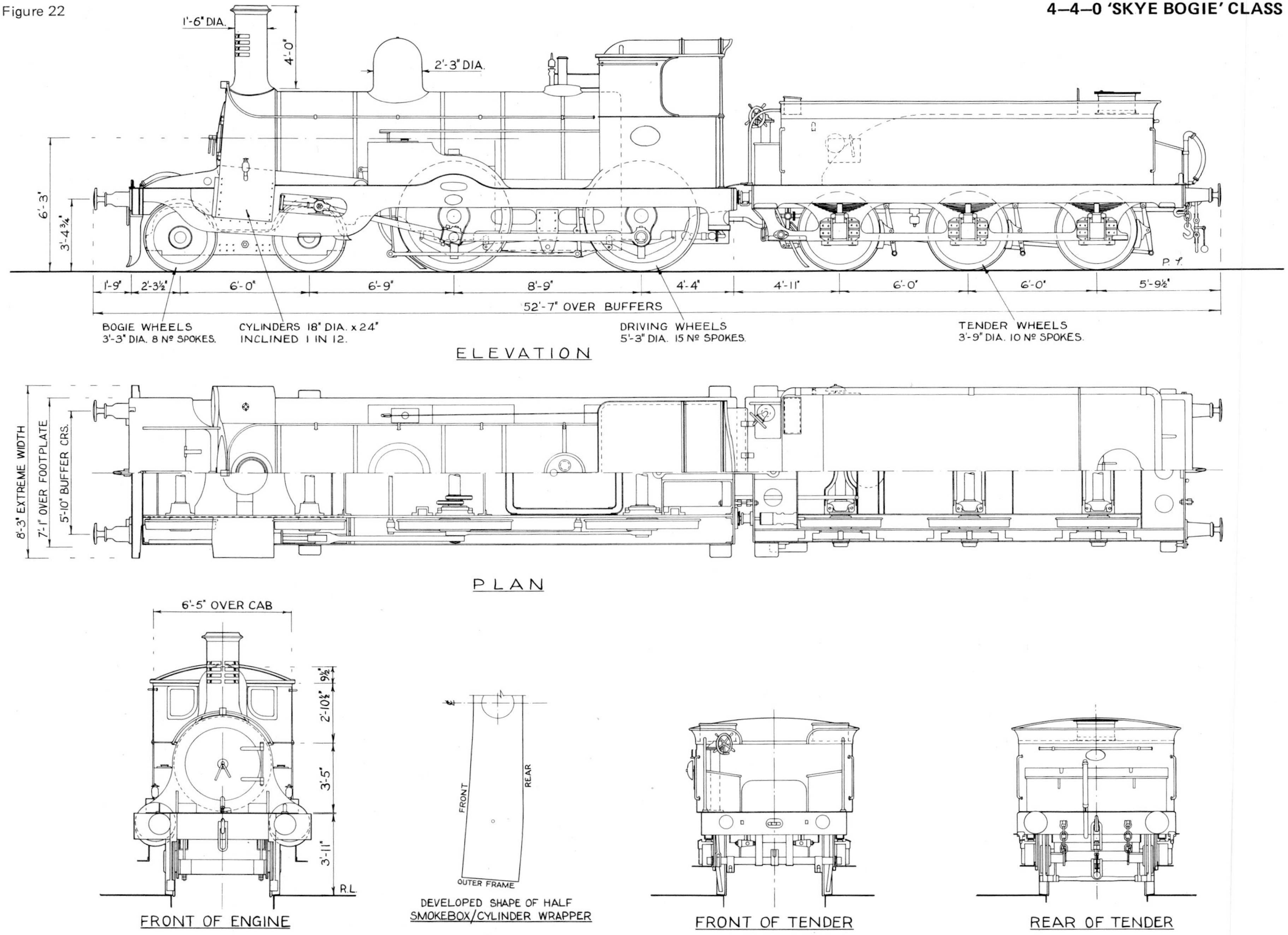

4–4–0 'SKYE BOGIE' CLASS

Plate 40

All members of the class lasted until grouping in 1923, although No. 85 failed to receive an LMS number and two more were never in fact applied, as plate 40 of No. 87 in June 1927 on the scrap line at Inverness demonstrates. Changes to the various fittings occurred over the years, of which the most significant was the tender exchanges usually for the 1,800 gallon variety from the 'Duke' class and plate 41 catches LMS No. 14277 ex No. 70 in this guise outside the timber engine shed at Dingwall.

4–4–0 'SKYE BOGIE' CLASS Total 9

HR No.	Built	LMS No.	Withdrawn	Remarks
70	5/82	14277	12/29	
85	8/92	–	8/23	Steel firebox fitted in 9/17 and replaced 11/22. Sold 12/23.
86	2/93	14279	10/27	
87	12/93	(14280)	12/26	
88	4/95	(14281)	12/26	
5	8/97	14282	9/29	
6	11/97	14283	8/29	Steel firebox replaced by copper 6/19
7	7/98	14284	4/30	
48	12/01	14285	10/28	

Renumbering:–

70 : 70A 12/12, 67 2/23
85 : 85A 4/18, 85 9/19, 85A 11/19
86 : 86A 4/18, 86 9/19

5 : 32 2/99
6 : 33 2/99
7 : 34 '99

Plate 41

Plate 42

Plate 43

Nos 5, 6, 7 and 48 did not appear until after Jones' resignation and possessed numerous Drummond features. A plain built up chimney and independent springing to the driving wheels, instead of the louvred double skin chimney and compensating beam and possible other minor modifications apparently effected a saving in building cost of more than 30 per cent, see appendix 14. No doubt Drummond, who had then recently taken up office, was keen to show that he was saving the company money and there is no suggestion that these latter locomotives were in any way inferior.

Plate 44

Drummond-built engines are illustrated on this page, plate 42 being of No. 33 on the turntable at Dingwall, whilst plates 43 and 44 also at Dingwall are of Nos 14284 in May 1928 and 14285 in LMS livery with the two varieties of tender and buffers.

4–4–0 'CLYDE BOGIE' CLASS

In a further development of the 'Duke' and 'Lochgorm Bogie' classes, the boilers of the 'Clyde Bogies' were pressed to 160 lb/sq in. The design of the frames and machinery was the same as the preceding 4–4–0 passenger classes, but the boiler was shorter and of two rings, while the firebox was correspondingly longer. The class derives its names from their builders the newly formed Clyde Locomotive Co. of Glasgow for whom these engines constituted the first order. No. 76 went to the Edinburgh Exhibition of 1886 and was not put into service until December that year.

Figure 23 shows the engines as built, while plate 45 is of Nos 79 ***Atholl*** (II) and 83 ***Monkland*** at Aviemore awaiting scrapping, having been worn out during the struggles of World War I.

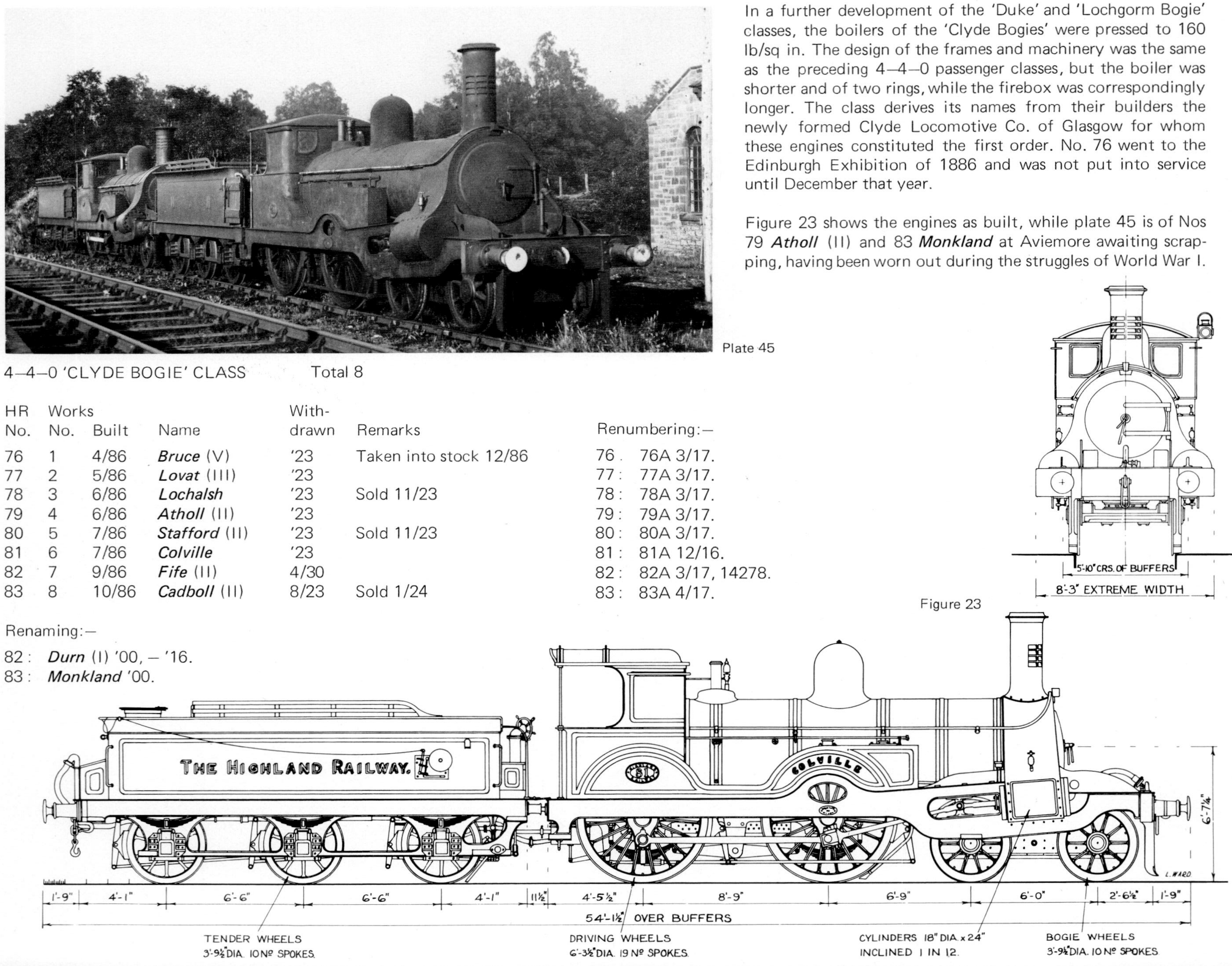

Plate 45

Figure 23

4–4–0 'CLYDE BOGIE' CLASS Total 8

HR No.	Works No.	Built	Name	With-drawn	Remarks
76	1	4/86	***Bruce*** (V)	'23	Taken into stock 12/86
77	2	5/86	***Lovat*** (III)	'23	
78	3	6/86	***Lochalsh***	'23	Sold 11/23
79	4	6/86	***Atholl*** (II)	'23	
80	5	7/86	***Stafford*** (II)	'23	Sold 11/23
81	6	7/86	***Colville***	'23	
82	7	9/86	***Fife*** (II)	4/30	
83	8	10/86	***Cadboll*** (II)	8/23	Sold 1/24

Renumbering:–

76 : 76A 3/17.
77 : 77A 3/17.
78 : 78A 3/17.
79 : 79A 3/17.
80 : 80A 3/17.
81 : 81A 12/16.
82 : 82A 3/17, 14278.
83 : 83A 4/17.

Renaming:–

82 : ***Durn*** (I) '00, – '16.
83 : ***Monkland*** '00.

Plate 46

The only one of the class to survive long enough to receive an LMS number and the crimson lake livery was No. 82 ***Durn*** (I) and this engine is to be seen in plate 46 as No. 14278 by then unnamed running round the branch train at Fochabers Town in May 1928. By this time a Drummond chimney had been fitted.

Plate 47

To replace the 2–2–2 tank No. 12 ***Strathpeffer*** (I) see page 16, Jones constructed at Lochgorm an 0–4–4 saddle tank making use of the boiler from No. 13 the only other member of the 'Belladrum' class, and of course named ***Strathpeffer*** (II) as illustrated in plate 47. In this form the engine lasted until 1901, when on renewal of the boiler opportunity was taken by Drummond to rebuild the engine with side tanks. Plate 48 shows the engine by now renumbered 53 in this form with driver J Stalker on the footplate.

Plate 48

0–4–4ST No. 13

Figure 24

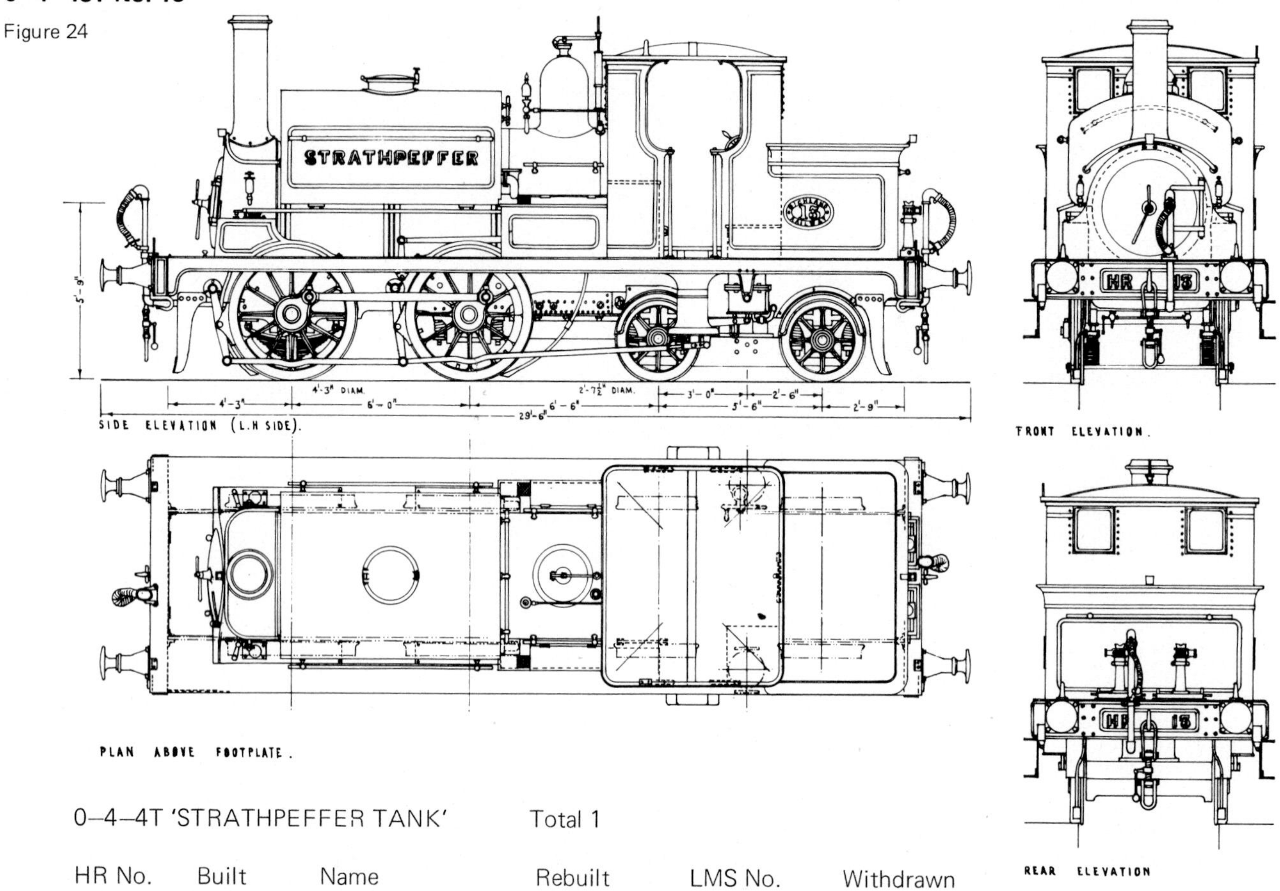

0–4–4T 'STRATHPEFFER TANK' Total 1

HR No.	Built	Name	Rebuilt	LMS No.	Withdrawn
13	5/90	*Strathpeffer* (II)	10/01	15050	12/29

Renaming:–
13 : *Lybster* 5/03.

Renumbering:–
13 : 53 9/99, 53A '19.

Plate 49

0–4–4ST No. 13

Figure 25

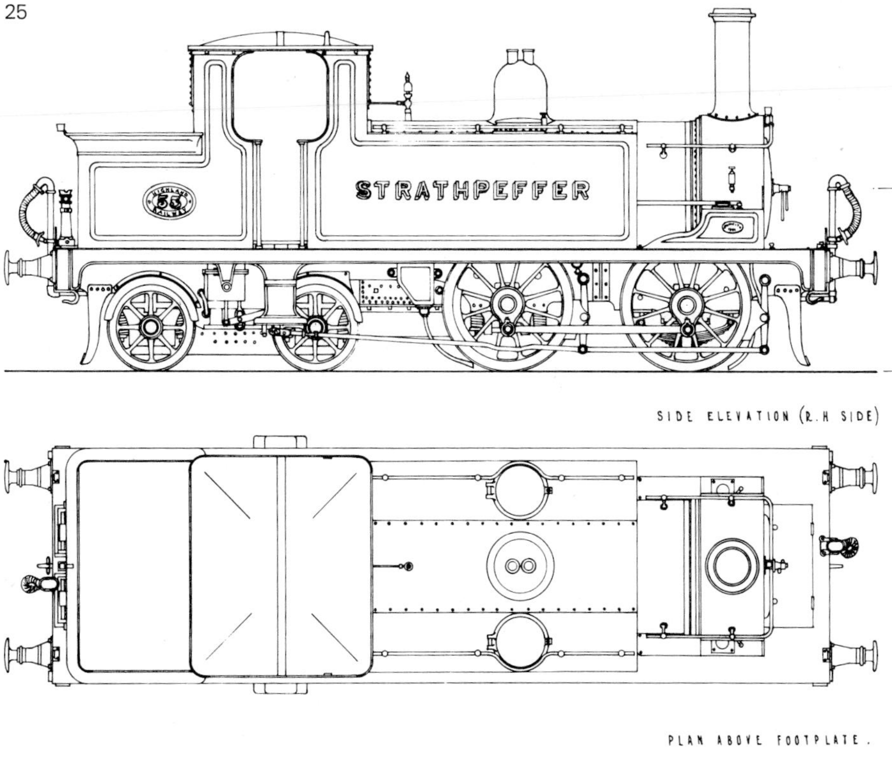

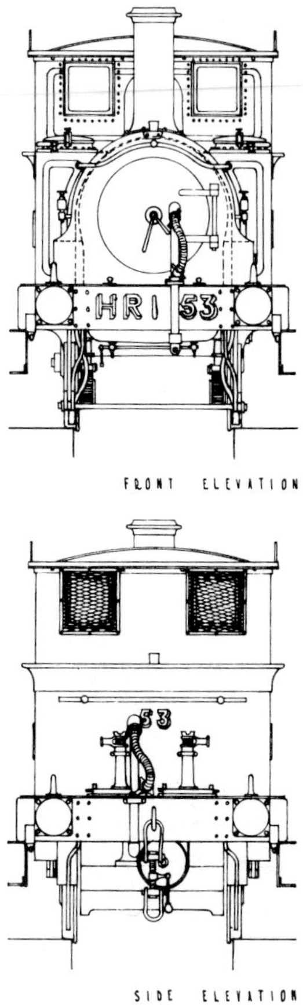

STRATHPEFFER

HR 53

6'-0"

SIDE ELEVATION (R.H SIDE)

FRONT ELEVATION

PLAN ABOVE FOOTPLATE.

SIDE ELEVATION

In 1903 this little engine was transferred to Wick to provide motive power on the newly opened Wick to Lybster light railway, and as plates 49 and 50 demonstrate it continued to perform this function for the LMS and received their number 15050 and the red livery. Both views were taken at Wick, the latter in May 1928. Figures 24 and 25 are drawings for the original and rebuilt versions respectively.

Plate 50

4–4–0 'STRATH' CLASS Total 12

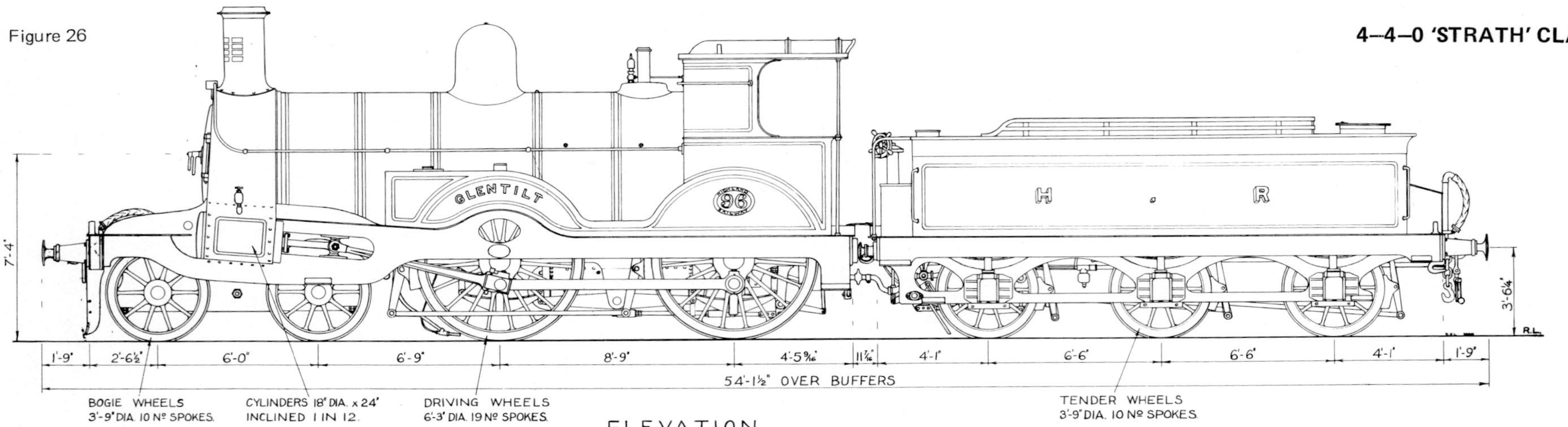

HR No.	Works No.	Built	Name	Steel firebox fitted	LMS No.	With-drawn	Remarks
89	4428	5/92	***Sir George***		14271	8/30	
90	4429	5/92	***Tweedale***		–	'23	Sold 12/23
91	4430	5/92	***Strathspey***	'16	–	'23	
92	4431	5/92	***Strathdearn***	'16	14272	2/30	
93	4432	6/92	***Strathnairn***	5/18	–	'23	Sold 12/23
94	4433	6/92	***Strathtay***		(14273)	3/25	
95	4434	6/92	***Strathcarron***	'21	14274	12/30	
96	4435	6/92	***Glentilt***	5/18	–	'23	Sold 12/23
97	4436	6/92	***Glenmore***	2/18	–	'23	Sold 12/23
98	4437	6/92	***Glentruim***	'20	14275	11/30	
99	4438	6/92	***Glentromie***	2/18	–	'23	Sold 12/23
100	4439	6/92	***Glenbruar***	'21	14276	2/30	

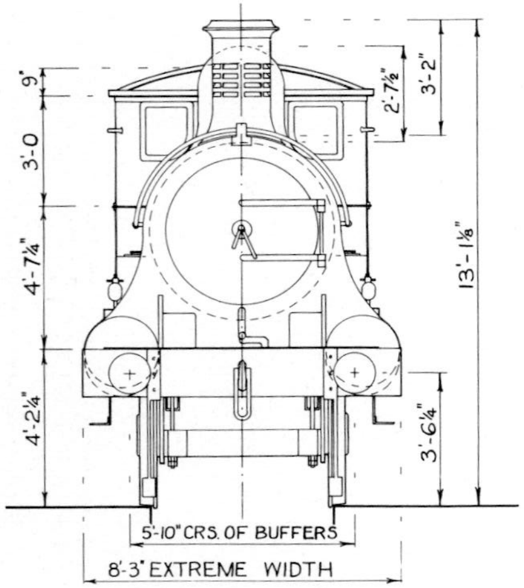

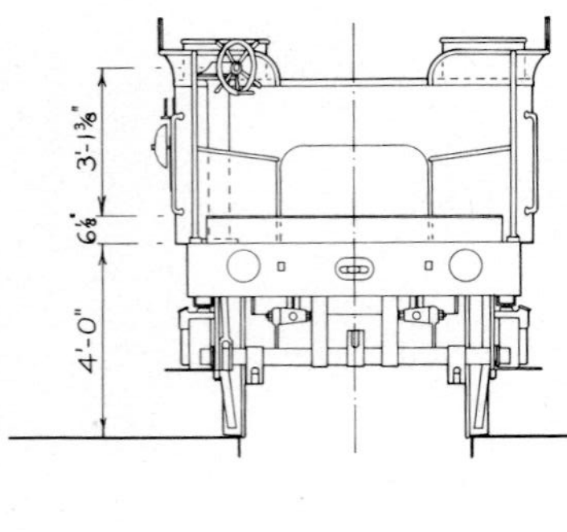

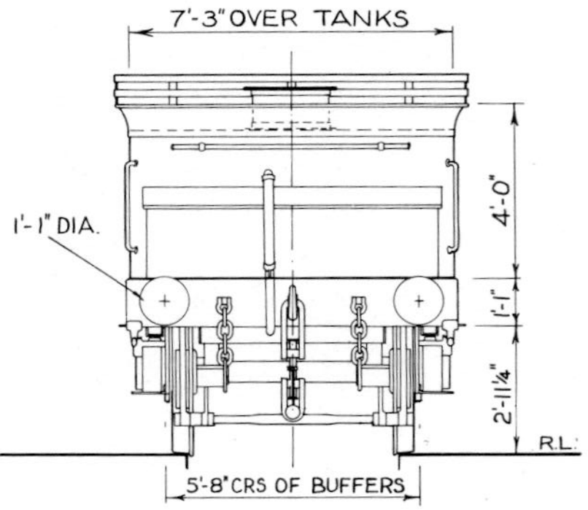

Renaming:–

90 : ***Grandtully*** '97.

Renumbering:–

89 : 89A 5/18, 89 9/19, 89A 11/19, 89 8/22.
90 : 90A 5/18, 90 9/19, 90A 11/19.
91 : 91A 6/18, 91 9/19, 91A 11/19.
92 : 92A 6/18, 92 8/18, 92A 4/19, 92 9/19, 92A 7/21.
93 : 93A 4/19, 93 9/19, 93A 8/21.
94 : 94A 4/19, 94 9/19.
95 : 95A 4/19, 95 9/19.
96 : 96A 4/19, 96 9/19, 96A 5/22.
97 : 97A 4/19, 97 9/19, 97A 5/22.
98 : 98A 7/19, 98 9/19.
99 : 99A 7/19, 99 9/19, 99A 8/22.
100 : 100A 7/19, 100 9/19.

4–4–0 'STRATH' CLASS

Plate 51

The 'Duke' class of 4–4–0 passenger engine and the developments in the form of the 'Lochgorm' and 'Clyde Bogies' having proved eminently satisfactory in service, Jones next mounted a larger boiler on the same design of frame, wheels and cylinders etc. to make the 'Strath' class built by Neilson Reid in 1892. In appearance these express passenger engines were rather massive for the period and lacked the gracefulness of the 'Duke' class.

Figure 26 opposite and plates 51 to 53 show various members of the class, the first photograph being of No. 90 ***Grandtully*** at Dingwall. Whereas this view is of an engine in Drummond's first livery style, the next two are of No. 98 ***Glentruim*** and No. 91 ***Strathspey*** in the later Jones scheme.

Plate 52

Plate 53

Plate 54

Plate 55

Plate 54 is another view of a 'Strath' at Dingwall, this time of No. 94 ***Strathtay***. Note the alarm bell on the tender side and the lamp above and right of the bell, together with the coal rails.

Plates 55 and 56 are both of No. 14272 ***Strathdearn*** in LMS crimson lake livery, the former at Forres in May 1928. The rear view of the tender is interesting in that it shows that the tool box above the buffers has been removed, as have the safety chains each side of the three link coupling, although the shackles are still apparent. The brass oil cups above each axle box should also be noticed.

The 'Straths' were the last class with double framing to be designed for the Highland Railway and their withdrawal, followed only by 'Jones Tank' No. 59, marked the end of this feature in Great Britain.

Plate 56

Plate 57

As can be seen from plate 57 No. 14274 ***Strathcarron*** received the LMS post 1928 lined black livery, together with a Drummond chimney cap, flatter dome and pop safety valves. In this photograph the engine is at Fochabers in May 1930.

As the name on the platform seat above the buffer beam proclaims, in plate 58 No. 14276 ***Glenbruar*** still in the red livery was photographed at Elgin in May 1928.

Plate 58

Plate 59

4–4–0T 'YANKEE TANK' CLASS Total 5

HR No.	Works No.	Taken into stock	Name – date (if any) applied		LMS No.	With-drawn	Remarks
101	2778	9/92	–	–	15013	7/34	
102	2779	9/92	*Munlochy*	'10	15014	12/34	Rebuilt in '06
11	3077	11/93	–	–	(15015)	5/24	
14	3078	11/93	*Portessie*	'01	15017	12/27	
15	3079	11/93	*Fortrose*	'01	15016	5/27	

Renumbering:–

101 : 101A 7/19, 101 8/22.
102 : 102A 7/19, 102 8/22.
11 : 51 7/98, 51A 12/16, 51B 8/22.
14 : 54 10/00, 54A 4/18, 54B 8/22.
15 : 52 12/00, 52A 3/17, 52B 8/22.

Plates 59 and 60 both show No. 101, the first in Jones livery and the addition of a lined timber screen to the cab cutout, whilst the second is at Dingwall after grouping although not yet repainted. Note the different positions and styles of the number plates.

Plate 60

The first two members of this class were built by Dübs and the parts for the remainder to hand originally for an order placed in December 1891 for the Uruguay Great Eastern Railway, but delivery was never accepted. After a trial period with the first two engines, the Highland Railway purchased them for use on branch lines and had the other three assembled with minor modifications to suit the new owner's needs. Despite the fact that Uruguay is part of the South American continent, these engines were commonly known as 'Yankee tanks'.

The three 4–4–0 tanks completed to Highland specifications had side tanks of increased capacity and a higher boiler pressure, although visually there is very little difference between the two batches as Plate 61 of No. 54 and figure 27 show.

4–4–0T 'YANKEE TANK' CLASS

1. Nos. 101 & 102

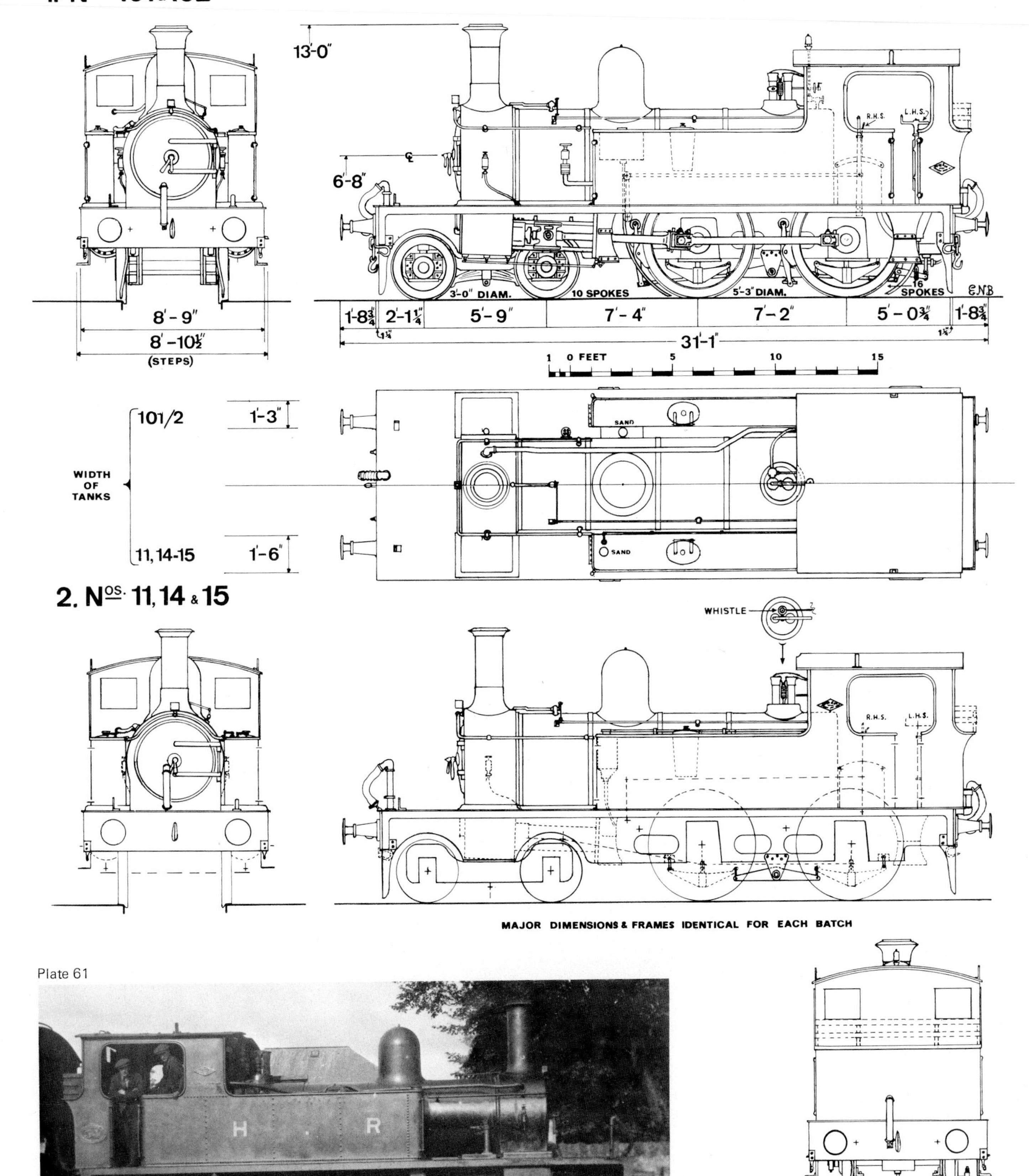

2. Nos. 11, 14 & 15

Plate 61

Figure 27

Plate 62

Plate 62 illustrates No. 15013 on the turntable at Wick in May 1928. Note the short Drummond buffers and packing at the front. In plate 63 No. 15014 is seen, together with Jones tank No. 15011, outside Lochgorm Works in May 1928 quite possibly awaiting attention to the leak chalked up on the bottom edge of the side tank. It is in its rebuilt form with Drummond boiler and fittings and was the only member of the class so treated.

Plate 63

4–6–0 'BIG GOODS' CLASS

Plate 64

Famous for being at the time of their introduction in 1894 the first British type to have a 4–6–0 wheel arrangement, Jones' 'Big Goods' class was rated as the most powerful main line engines in Britain, a claim which they were able to prove amply in service. They were at the time the heaviest locomotives in the country and formed a striking departure from current locomotive practice.

Two are seen in plate 64 moving off from Inverness shed in 1901, with the front ends of No. 57 ***Lochgorm*** in the background and No. 100 ***Glenbruar*** to the left hand side. In plate 65 No. 111 is pictured in winter time quite possibly soon after delivery from the builders, Sharp Stewart now of Glasgow, as no tablet exchange apparatus has yet been fitted.

4–6–0 'BIG GOODS' CLASS Total 15

HR No.	Works No.	Built	LMS No.	With-drawn	Remarks
103	4022	9/94	17916	7/34	Preserved at Glasgow Museum of Transport
104	4023	9/94	17917	11/39	
105	4024	9/94	17918	5/33	
106	4025	9/94	17919	3/34	Westinghouse brake
107	4026	9/94	17920	10/37	
108	4027	9/94	17921	11/30	
109	4028	10/94	17922	9/29	Steel fb 11/17, Copper 8/21
110	4029	10/94	17923	11/35	
111	4030	10/94	17924	10/34	
112	4031	10/94	17925	2/40	
113	4032	10/94	17926	11/39	
114	4033	10/94	17927	9/36	
115	4034	11/94	17928	5/33	
116	4035	11/94	17929	6/36	Westinghouse brake until '34
117	4036	11/94	17930	11/39	

Plate 65

Figure 28

4–6–0 'BIG GOODS' CLASS

1'-6⅝" 1'-8⅛" 6'-9½" 10'-10"
1'-7" DIA.
3'-0"
2'-6⅜"
1'-5½" 2'-2⅜" 13'-3" 1'-4⅜" 1'-8¼" 1'-2½"
7'-4"
3'-6¼"
3'-6¼"
R.L.
1'-9" 2'-4" 3'-3" 3'-3" 5'-3" 5'-6" 7'-9" 5'-8" 8½" 4'-1" 6'-6" 6'-6" 4'-1" 1'-9"
58'-4½" OVER BUFFERS

BOGIE WHEELS 3'-2½" DIA. 8 Nº SPOKES.

CYLINDERS 20" DIA. x 26" INCLINED 1 IN 24.

DRIVING WHEELS 5'-3½" DIA. 15 Nº SPOKES.

TENDER WHEELS 3'-9½" DIA. 10 Nº SPOKES.

ELEVATION

5'-10" CRS. OF BUFFERS
5'-8" CRS. OF BUFFERS

PLAN

7'-0" OVER CAB
13'-0"
9⅛" 3'-0" ½" 3'-6¼" 4'-5⅞"
R.L.

FRONT OF ENGINE

8'-6" OVER COPING

FRONT OF TENDER

7'-9" OVER TANK
1'-4¼" 3'-10¾" 4'-0⅝"
R.L.

REAR OF TENDER

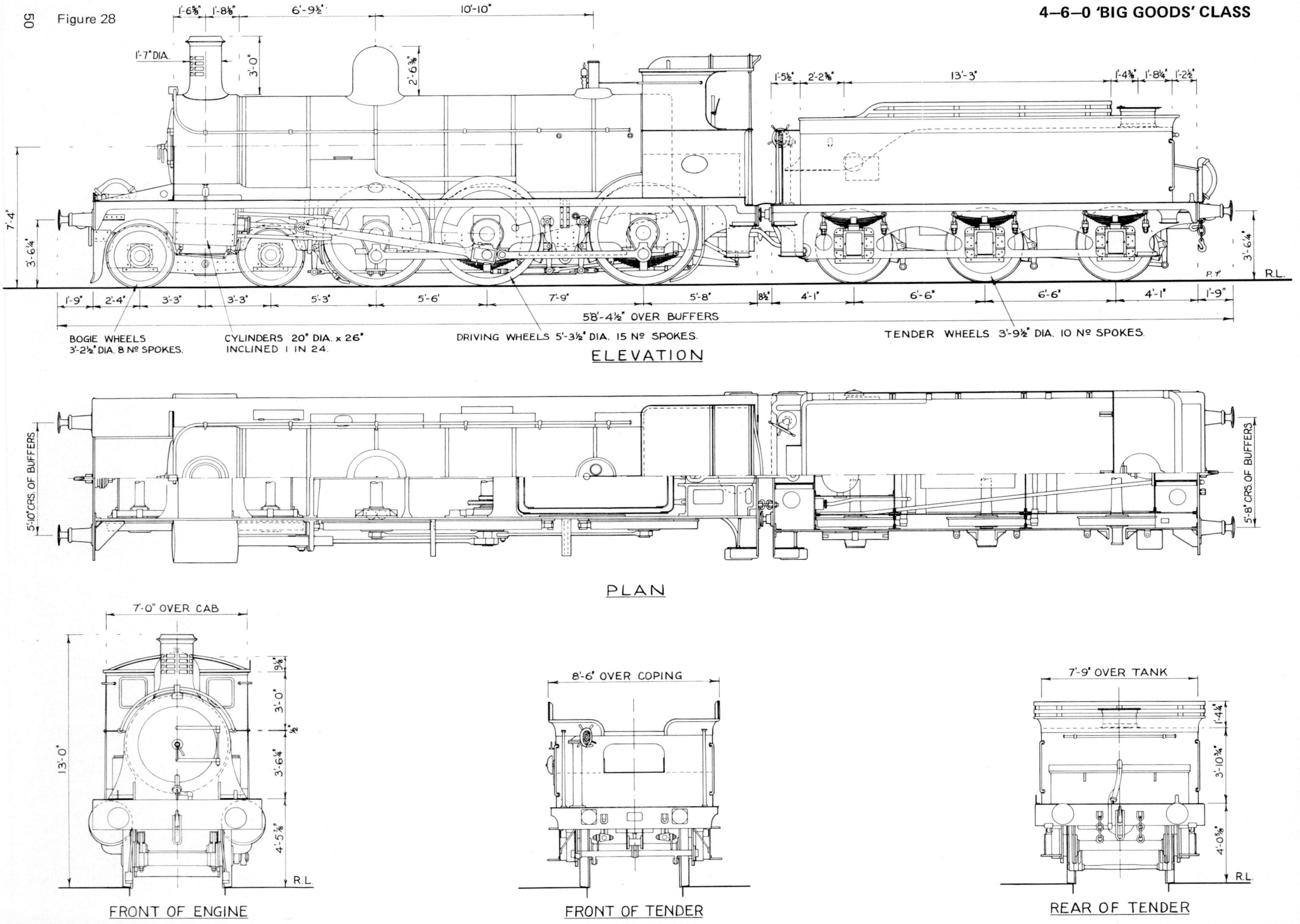

4–6–0 'BIG GOODS' CLASS

A drawing of the class in original condition is reproduced in figure 28 opposite. Note that the middle set of driving wheels were flangeless. While plate 66 shows No. 108 in work shop grey outside Lochgorm Works fitted with a large snow plough, which involved adding a lamp bracket half way up the chimney. Again in Jones II livery plate 67 depicts No. 116 at Perth having recently been cleaned and wiped with an oily rag in the elaborate style fashionable at the time.

Plate 66

Plate 67

Plate 68

The 'Big Goods' continued to do good work on the Highland Section under LMS ownership and in plate 68 No. 17928 is seen at Inverness in May 1930 sporting a '4F' power classification on the upper cab side and a lined livery really intended for passenger engines. Note how the rails almost intersect at the circumference to the turntable. In plate 69 No. 17930, also still carrying a louvred chimney but Ross pop safety valves, is starting a northbound through freight past Welsh's Bridge Junction signal cabin, Inverness again in May 1930.

Plate 69

Plate 70

Plate 71

To more recent generations the Highland locomotive is exemplified by the preserved No. 103. This engine was first set aside by the LMS, when as No. 17916 it was withdrawn from revenue earning service in 1934 and plate 70 depicts the engine following its first restoration in 1935/6. At this time it was painted in a green livery, retaining pop safety valves and still without wing plates or flanged middle wheels.

Plate 71 illustrates the condition in which most members of the class ended their days with Drummond chimneys and smokebox wing plates removed, although strangely No. 17923 still has the original type of safety valve. It also has an enlarged tender. Some engines were fitted with flanges to the middle wheels and from May 1934 frequently worked on the Skye line.

In 1959 No. 103 was placed in working order and, along with several other famous Scottish preserved engines, used to haul enthusiasts' specials until seven years later they were placed on static exhibit at the Glasgow Museum of Transport. During this Indian summer No. 103 was, and still is at the time of writing, adorned in a hybrid dark yellow livery. Plate 72 of the cab interior was taken at Aviemore during a memorable three day tour of the Highland lines in June 1962, organised jointly by the Stephenson Locomotive Society and Railway Correspondence and Travel Society.

Plate 72

2–4–0T 'SPECIAL TANK'

This engine was originally supplied by Kitson to the third Duke of Sutherland for use on his railway, first opened between Dunrobin and West Helmsdale in November 1870 and at that time not yet connected to the Highland system. A diagram of the engine in its original condition is reproduced in figure 29.

Figure 29

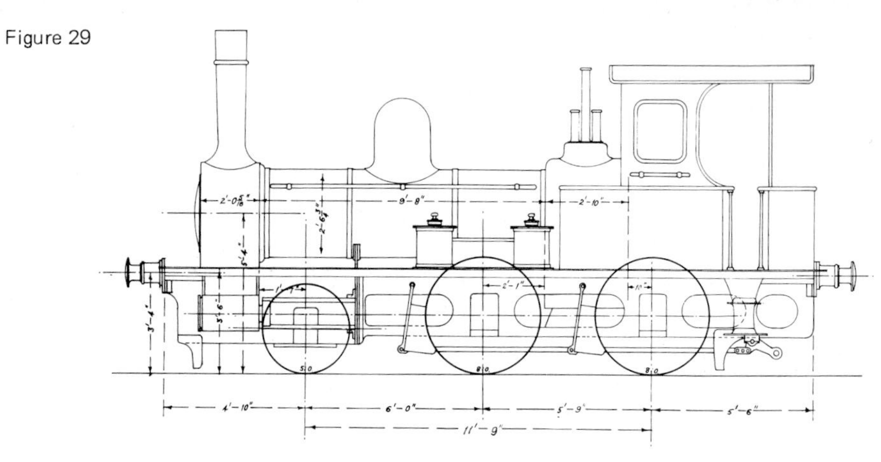

2–4–0T 'SPECIAL TANK'   Total 1

HR No.	Works No.	Built	Taken into HR stock	Name	Rebuilt	With-drawn	Remarks
118	1706	'70	11/95	***Dunrobin*** (I)	5/96	'23	Sold c.'23

Renaming:–

118 : *Gordon Castle* (I) '96, – '00.

Renumbering:–

118 : 118A 7/13.

Figure 30

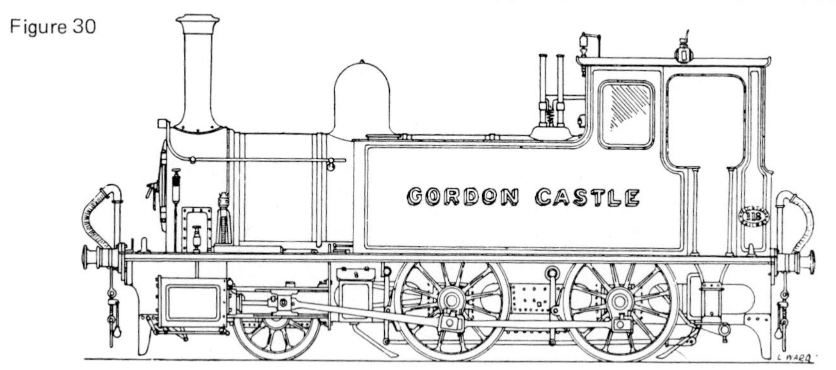

On the Duke's death his son decided on a new engine and the Highland Railway was prevailed upon to purchase the 1870 engine for the sum of £300. Another £1,364 was then paid to have Sharp Stewart's rebuild it with a new boiler and larger cylinders in the form shown in figure 30 and plate 73.

Plate 73

0–4–4T 'DUNROBIN' (II)

Plate 74

The Duke of Sutherland's new engine of course was never part of the Highland stock or indeed its successors, but it is so obviously associated with the line that no apology is made for including it. Designed by Jones and built by Sharp Stewart it remained in the Sutherlands' hands until on nationalisation its further use on the main line was prevented. After a sojourn on England's south coast, it was shipped to Canada where it is understood to be on display.

0–4–4T 'DUNROBIN' (II) Total 1

Works No.	Built	Name	Sold to:	Date	Location
4085	7/95	*Dunrobin* (II)	i Capt. Howey	'49	New Romney, Kent.
			ii Imperial Pagents Ltd.	3/65	Victoria, British Columbia.
			iii Govt. of British Columbia	11/65	Fort Steel, British Columbia.

Plate 74 illustrates ***Dunrobin*** (II) in balmier days on the north side of Inverness station complete with the Duke's own special saloon built at Wolverton in 1899, while figure 31 shows some of the technical aspects of the engine.

Figure 31

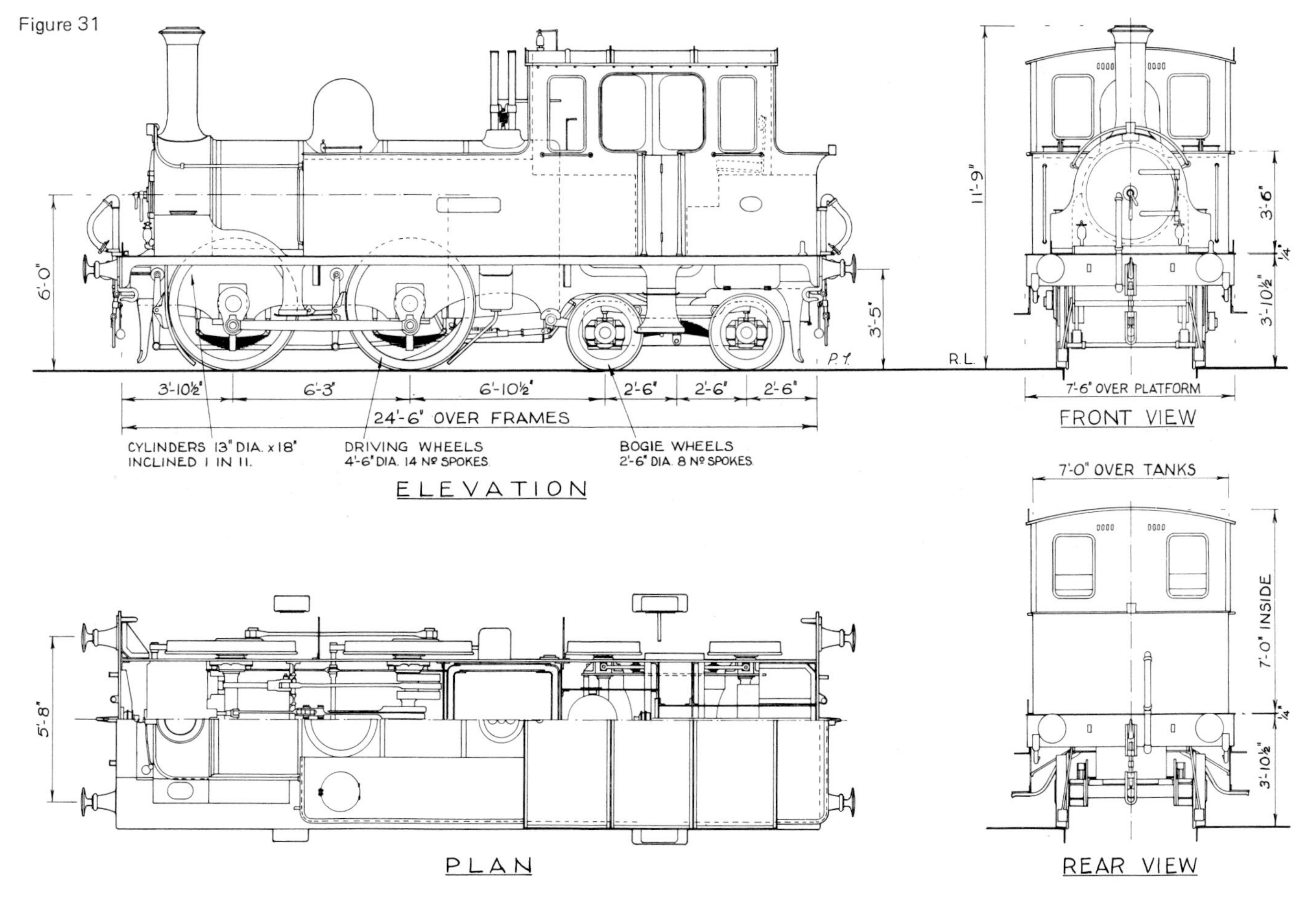

4–4–0 'LOCH' CLASS

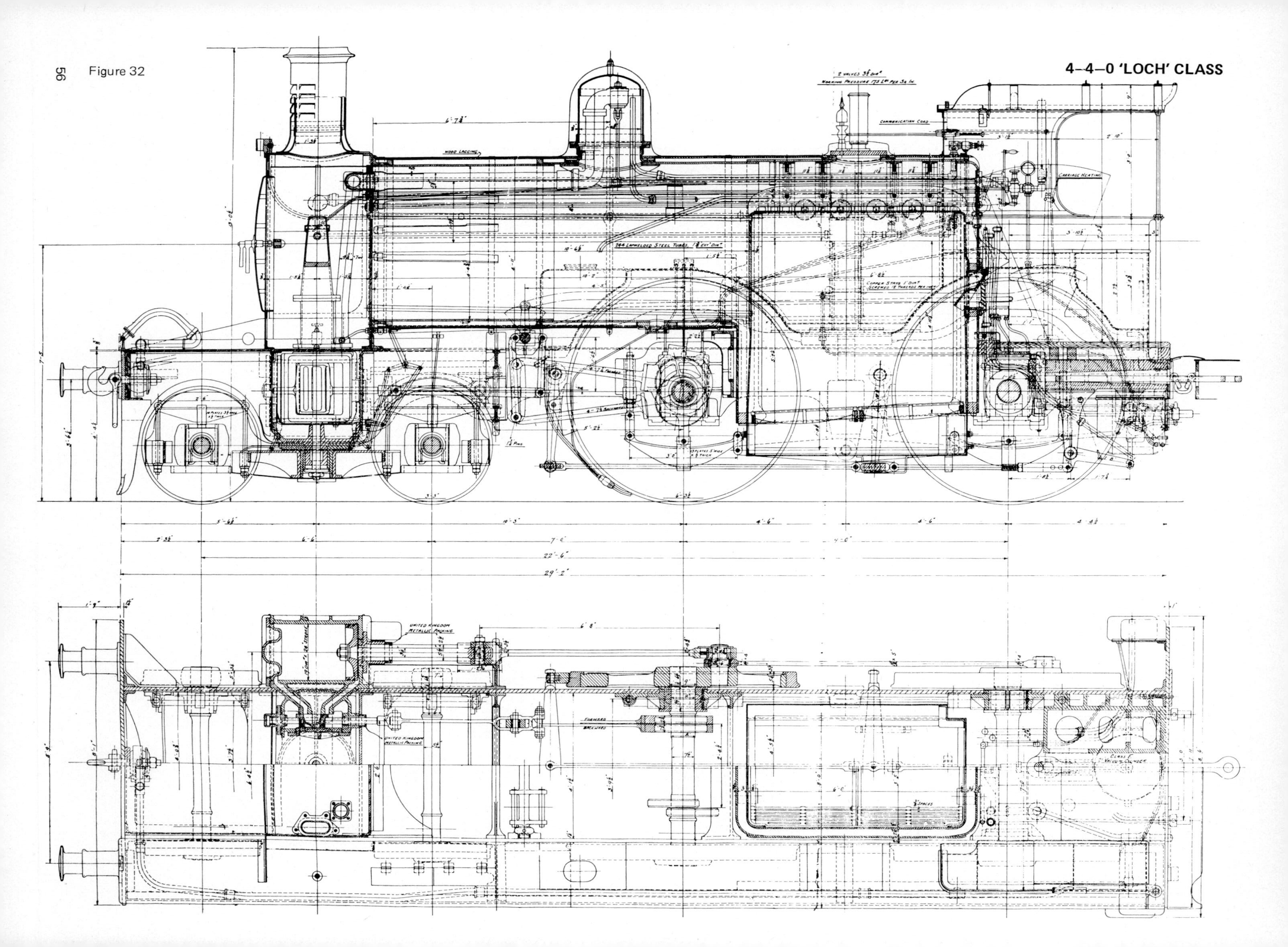

Figure 32

Plate 75

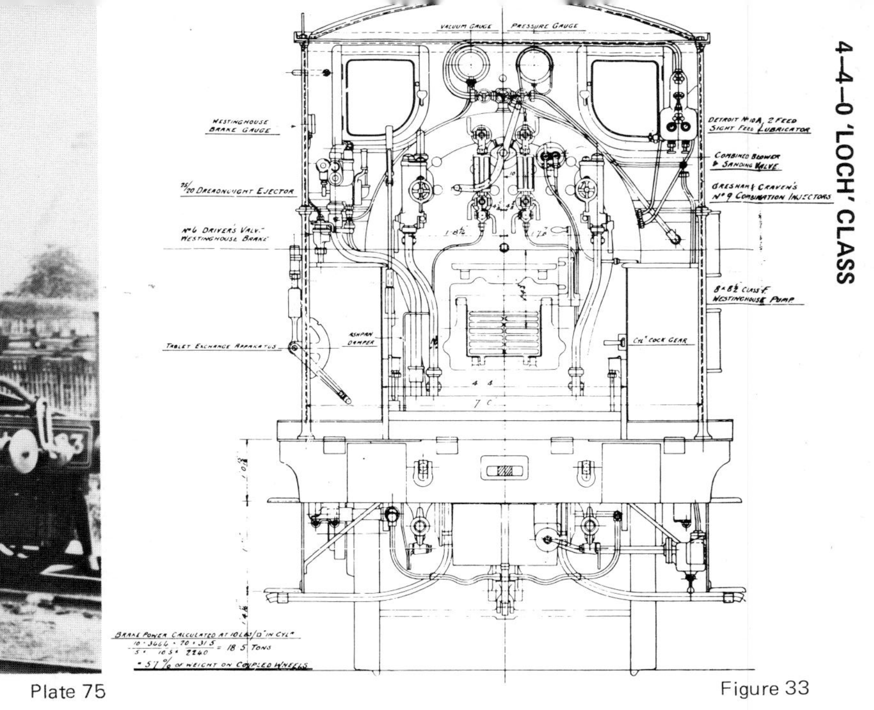

Figure 33

This was the last class of engine designed by David Jones. They were for express passenger work and possessed many of the features first seen on the 'Big Goods' class. They were among the earliest engines in the country to be fitted with piston valves, being of the W M Smith patent. This particular type of valve did not prove altogether satisfactory and was replaced from 1899 onwards by Richardson balanced slide valves.

Figures 32 and 33 are taken from the general arrangement drawing of the 1917 batch, the tender to the original order being exactly the same as the 'Big Goods' tender with the addition of side doors. Nos 121 and 132 had their tool boxes removed and the tanks extended, whilst those delivered in 1917 had the larger capacity tenders from the outset. Plate 75 shows No. 123 ***Loch an Dorb*** in Drummond (I) livery.

4–4–0 'LOCH' CLASS Total 18

HR No.	Builder	Works No.	Built	Name	LMS No.	Reboilered	With-drawn	Remarks
119	Dübs	3392	7/96	***Loch Insh***	14379	'25	3/48	
120	Dübs	3393	7/96	***Loch Ness***	14380	'28	11/41	
121	Dübs	3394	8/96	***Loch Ericht***	14381	'24	3/40	
122	Dübs	3395	8/96	***Loch Moy***	14382	'26	12/40	
123	Dübs	3396	8/96	***Loch an Dorb***	14383	'28	12/34	
124	Dübs	3397	8/96	***Loch Laggan***	14384	–	9/38	
125	Dübs	3398	8/96	***Loch Tay***	14385	'28	4/50	
126	Dübs	3399	8/96	***Loch Tummel***	14386	'28	8/38	
127	Dübs	3400	8/96	***Loch Garry***	14387	–	12/30	
128	Dübs	3401	8/96	***Loch Luichart***	14388	–	12/30	
129	Dübs	3402	9/96	***Loch Maree***	14389	–	2/31	
130	Dübs	3403	9/96	***Loch Fannich***	14390	'25	2/37	Fitted with feed water heater 10/13
131	Dübs	3404	9/96	***Loch Shin***	14391	9/24	8/41	Used as bombing target at Shoeburyness
132	Dübs	3405	9/96	***Loch Navar***	14392	'27	4/47	
133	Dübs	3406	9/96	***Loch Laoghal***	14393	–	12/34	
70	NB Loco	21456	3/17	***Loch Ashie***	14394	–	9/36	Westinghouse brake
71	NB Loco	21457	3/17	***Loch Garve***	14395	–	11/35	Westinghouse brake
72	NB Loco	21458	3/17	***Loch Ruthven***	14396	–	10/34	Westinghouse brake

Renaming:–

119 : 8/44, ***Loch Insh*** '46.
133 : ***Loch Laochal*** c'30.

Plate 76

Plate 77

A further three liveries are apparent in plate 76 to 78. The first is of No. 124 ***Loch Laggan*** at Stanley Junction in the Jones (II) scheme. The stripes of tallow on the engine axle ends are to detect hot journals and indicate that the engine is on delivery from the builders. The photograph once belonged to the young man with his foot on the tender sand box. No. 131 ***Loch Shin*** is seen in Smith livery, with number painted on the cab side, at Kyle engine shed; while No. 127 ***Loch Garry*** was photographed at Perth in August 1925 in Cummings' style, although retaining its original number plate.

Plate 78

4–4–0 'LOCH' CLASS

Plate 79

Three of Mr Casserley's photographs of 'Lochs' all in the LMS crimson lake livery with black and pale yellow lining, large gold letters on the tender and crest on the cab side are reproduced on this page. Plate 79 illustrates No. 14387 ***Loch Garry*** at Perth in May 1928. Plate 80 is of No. 14389 ***Loch Maree*** alongside the old coaling stage at Inverness in June 1927, while in plate 81 No. 14393 ***Loch Laochal*** pauses at Dalnaspidal prior to returning to Blair Atholl for further banking duties in May 1928. Note how the name of the second two is on a radius concentric with the forward driving wheel centre and the first is on a larger radius curve. No. 14393's chimney has also been cut down and flatter dome fitted.

Plate 80

Plate 81

Plate 82

Plate 83

The first signs of the LMS' more down to earth approach to overhauls can be seen in the snap head rivets to the renewed smokebox and the cast iron chimney on No. 14384 ***Loch Laggan*** in plate 82.

Plate 83 illustrates No. 14384 ***Loch Laggan*** again in May 1928 on shed at Blair Atholl. Note that the tool box at the rear of the tender has been removed.

Plate 84

The LMS scheme for standardisation of boilers on the Northern Division resulted in the fitting of CR '812' class boilers to the 'Lochs', which, as may be seen from plate 84 of No. 14391 ***Loch Shin***, rather drastically altered their appearance for the worse. However this course of action did prolong the life of the class, two of which lasted to be absorbed into British Railways.

4–4–0 'SMALL BEN' CLASS

The first design introduced by Peter Drummond was a class of 4–4–0s named after mountains in the territory served by the Company. These engines were very neat and graceful in appearance and were popular with the enginemen. Although slightly less powerful than the 'Loch' class, they proved their worth on the Inverness-Wick and Inverness-Keith sections, whereon they were used extensively. Whereas the cost of building the 'Lochs' was charged to the capital account, thereby receiving fresh running numbers and at the time of their introduction put to work on the principal express services, the provision of the 'Bens' was considered as the renewal of some of the early Allan engines, the expenditure being set against revenue and the old numbers reused. To obtain a reasonably continuous run a few old engines still lingering on were renumbered to make way for the 'Bens'.

All except the last three were originally coupled to 3,000 gallon tenders, as drawn overleaf in figure 34; 3,185 gallon tenders being provided for Nos 38, 41 and 47. Nos 2, 13, 15 and 17 exchanged tenders with four from 'Barneys' of the 3,200 gallon bogie type, whilst Nos 1 and 6 had their small tenders enlarged before grouping in 1923, after which further changes seem to have taken place.

Plate 85

In plate 85 No. 38 *Ben Udlaman* is on the turntable at Keith in August 1925 still in Highland livery. During an overhaul, probably at a foreign works during the latter part or after World War I, Cumming apparently had the safety valves repositioned from the dome to the firebox.

4–4–0 'SMALL BEN' CLASS Total 20

HR No.	Builder	Works No.	Built	Name	LMS No.	N34 boiler carried	With-drawn	Remarks
1	Dübs	3685	7/98	*Ben Nevis*	14397	'28	2/49	BR No. 54397
2	Dübs	3686	7/98	*Ben Alder*	14398	11/29	2/53	Westinghouse brake until 2/17 BR No. 54398
3	Dübs	3687	7/98	*Ben Wyvis*	14399	'27	4/52	BR No. 54399
4	Dübs	3688	2/99	*Ben More*	14400	'27	10/46	
5	Dübs	3689	2/99	*Ben Vrackie*	14401	'29	11/48	
6	Dübs	3690	2/99	*Ben Armin*	14402	'27	12/39	Steel fb 2/19
7	Dübs	3691	2/99	*Ben Attow*	14403	'27	2/49	
8	Dübs	3692	2/99	*Ben Clebrig*	14404	'28	10/50	BR No. 54404
9	Lochgorm		7/99	*Ben Rinnes*	14405	'27	9/44	
10	Lochgorm		9/99	*Ben Slioch*	14406	'30	7/47	
11	Lochgorm		11/99	*Ben Macdhui*	14407	—	4/31	
12	Lochgorm		4/00	*Ben Hope*	14408	'27	7/47	Steel fb 12/18 Westinghouse brake
13	Lochgorm		6/00	*Ben Alisky*	14409	'28	4/50	Westinghouse brake
14	Lochgorm		8/00	*Ben Dearg*	14410	'28	12/49	Westinghouse brake
15	Lochgorm		2/01	*Ben Loyal*	14411	—	10/36	Westinghouse brake
16	Lochgorm		2/01	*Ben Avon*	14412	'28	4/47	Westinghouse brake
17	Lochgorm		2/01	*Ben Alligan*	14413	—	12/33	Westinghouse brake
38	NB Loco	17398	8/06	*Ben Udlaman*	14414	—	12/33	
41	NB Loco	17399	7/06	*Ben Bharch Ard*	14415	'28	5/48	
47	NB Loco	17400	7/06	*Ben a' Bhuird*	14416	'27	9/48	

Renaming:—

1 : *Ben-y-Gloe* 7/98, *Ben y-Gloe* , *Ben y'Gloe* '39.

Figure 34

4–4–0 'SMALL BEN' CLASS

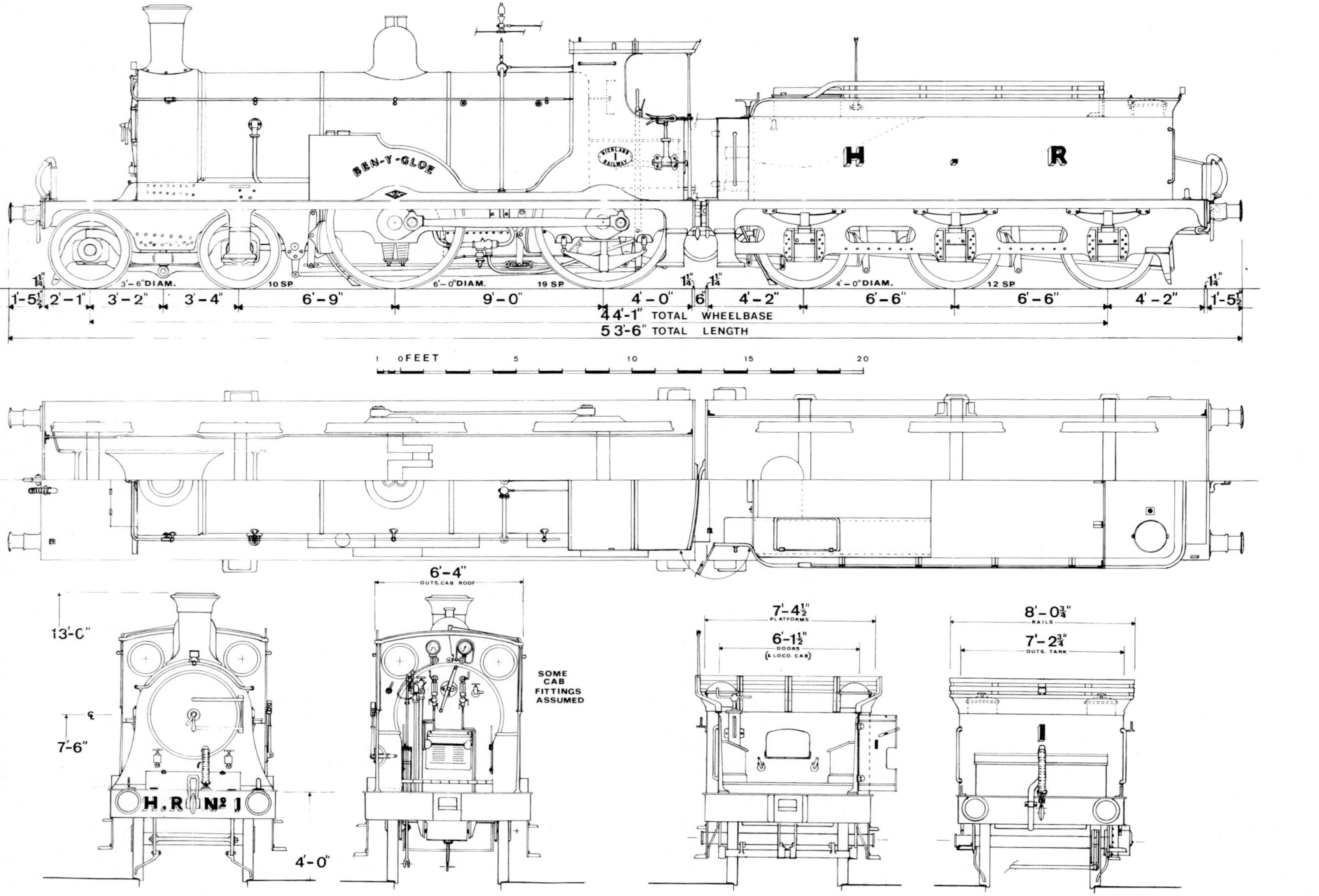

Plate 86

Plate 87

Plates 86 and 87 illustrate Dübs and Lochgorm built versions of the 'Ben' class, being No. 1 ***Ben-y-Gloe*** and No. 12 ***Ben Hope.*** Both are in the highly polished Drummond I livery, although the immaculate state of No. 1 suggests it is not long out of the builder's paint shop. This photograph also shows the underslung reach rod passing under and behind the driving wheels, together with the reversing lever upon which the driver is resting his hand. No. 9 onwards were built with steam reversing gear and the earlier engines altered to conform.

Plate 88

No. 14398 *Ben Alder* in LMS lined black livery and coupled to a bogie 8 wheeled tender is depicted in plate 88 standing at the head of a north bound train at Dingwall. Like No. 38 in plate 85 the safety valves are on the firebox, but otherwise the engine is generally in original condition. The tender however has had steps added at the rear.

In plate 89 No. 14404 *Ben Clebrig* still had a Highland boiler when photographed outside Dingwall shed in May 1928. This locomotive is in the earlier LMS crimson lake livery for passenger engines.

Plate 89

Plate 90

As the list on page 61 records from 1927 all but four of the class were reboilered with the CR standard goods boiler and modified pattern 'Dunalastair' 18¼ by 26 inch cylinders. Plate 90 showing No. 14408 ***Ben Hope*** at Forres in June 1937 is in this condition. Notice also that the wing plates have been removed and a Caley chimney and smokebox door fitted.

Plate 91 illustrates No. 14413 ***Ben Alligan*** at Blair Atholl in May 1928 having arrived with the slow train from Perth. The holes in the buffer beam are for attaching a snow plough in winter and, as other photographs show, heavy angle irons were frequently fitted at other times of the year.

Plate 91

Plate 92

A valiant attempt was made to preserve the last 'Small Ben', which by then was British Railways No. 54398 ***Ben Alder***, and the locomotive was held in store for many years while various feasibility studies for her official restoration were undertaken. The problem was that it was not practical at an economic price to restore her to original condition and working order, although the possibility of fitting a boiler from a Dugald Drummond designed LSWR 0–4–4T 'M7' class was investigated. On the failure of these plans to mature and an abortive attempt at private preservation, the engine was reluctantly sent to the scrap heap in April 1966. When one considers the numerous rusting heaps that only a few years later were to be rescued and lovingly restored, it can only be regretted that ***Ben Alder*** is not with us today to work on, say, the Strathspey Railway from Aviemore to Boat of Garten, even if to be historically correct it had to be in LMS livery.

Plate 92 is of ***Ben Alder*** during the engine's last days and plates 93 and 94 close ups of the footplate and tender.

Plate 93

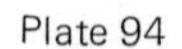

Plate 94

0–6–0 'BARNEY' CLASS

Plate 95

The 'Barney' class was designed for goods traffic and had boilers and cylinders which were interchangeable with those of the 'Small Ben' class. The first six engines supplied had bogie 8 wheeled tenders, but these were subsequently exchanged for the 6 wheeled pattern. Nos 18 to 21 had water tube fireboxes until removed by the LMS. All engines were vacuum brake fitted on being built, thus enabling them to work passenger trains when required, which they frequently did. The front vacuum pipe was foreshortened to allow the smokebox door to open fully.

Plate 95 depicts No. 37 outside Wick shed in August 1923 and a drawing for the class will be found as figure 35 overleaf.

0–6–0 'BARNEY' CLASS Total 12

HR No.	Builder	Works No.	Built	Tenders capacity (gallons) as built	replacement	date	LMS No.	Water tubes (if any) removed	N 34 boiler carried	Withdrawn	Remarks
134	Dübs	3842	2/00	3,200	3,000	3/06	17693	–	'26	6/49	HR boiler refitted 2/36 to 8/42
135	Dübs	3843	2/00	3,200	3,000	4/10	17694	–	'37	2/50	
136	Dübs	3844	2/00	3,200	3,000	u/k	17695	–	'31	1/52	HR boiler refitted 3/44 to 5/48. BR No. 57695
137	Dübs	3845	2/00	3,200	3,000	8/09	17696	–	8/42	3/46	Tender extended 4/10
138	Dübs	3846	2/00	3,200	3,185	4/10	17697	–	8/35	2/51	BR No. 57697
139	Dübs	3847	2/00	3,200	3,185	12/09	17698	–	9/31	12/51	HR boiler refitted 11/35 BR No. 57698
18	Dübs	4240	8/02	3,000	–	–	17699	'24	3/43	2/49	
19	Dübs	4241	8/02	3,000	–	–	17700	'25	8/31	12/46	
20	Dübs	4242	8/02	3,000	–	–	17701	'23	–	2/36	
21	Dübs	4243	8/02	3,000	–	–	17702	'34	5/36	11/49	HR boiler refitted 1/43
36	NB Loco	17896	7/07	3,185	–	–	17703	–	'37	7/47	Steel fb '19
55	NB Loco	17897	7/07	3,185	–	–	17704	–	10/31	12/46	

Renumbering:–

55 : 37 8/21

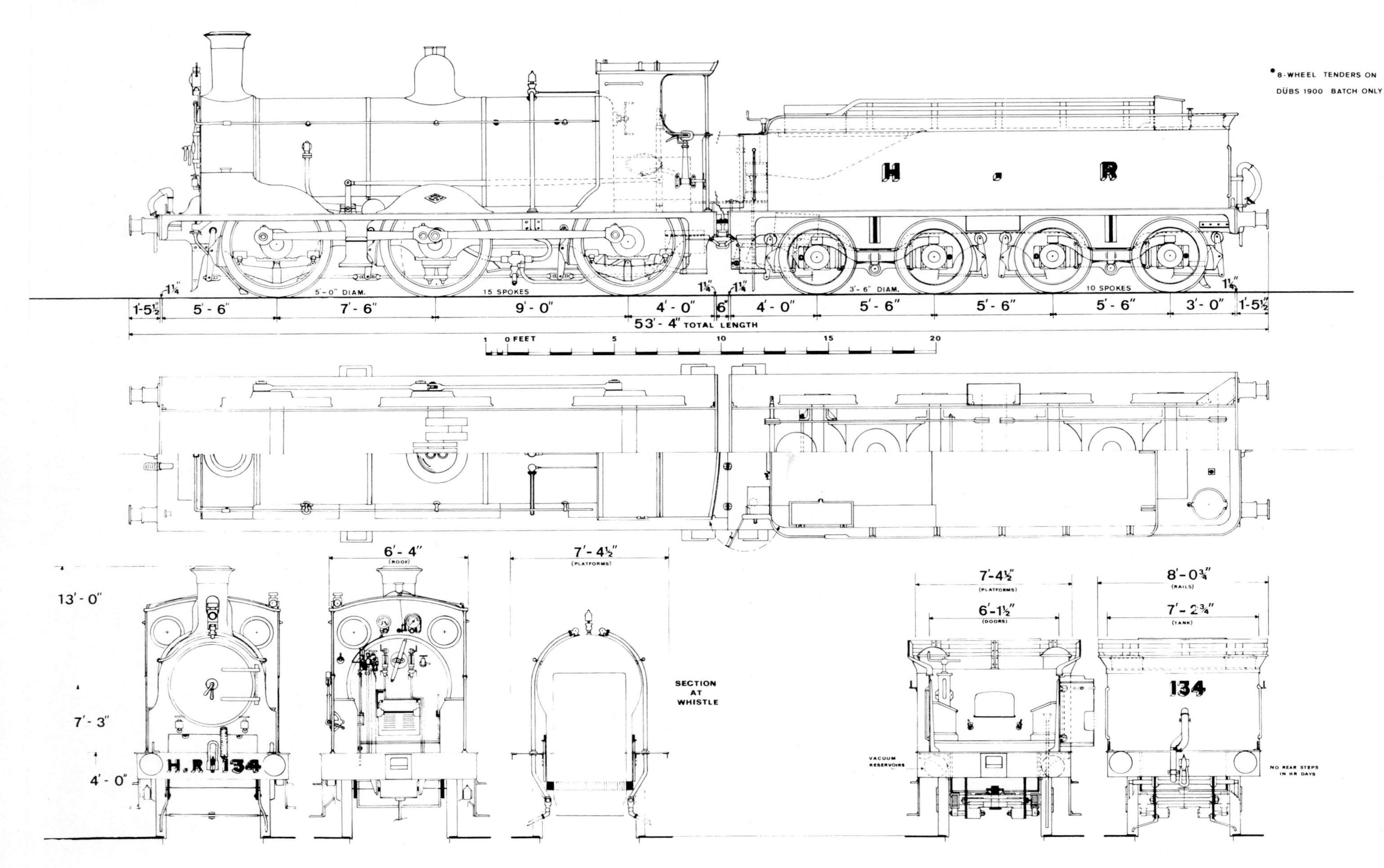
HIGHLAND RAILWAY P. DRUMMOND 'BARNEY' 0-6-0
BUILT BY DÜBS & CO. 1900*/1902; N.B.L. CO. 1907 © E.N. BELLASS 1978
*8-WHEEL TENDERS ON DÜBS 1900 BATCH ONLY
H R
5'-0" DIAM.
15 SPOKES
3'-6" DIAM.
10 SPOKES
1¼"
1'-5½"
5'-6"
7'-6"
9'-0"
4'-0"
6"
4'-0"
5'-6"
5'-6"
5'-6"
3'-0"
1'-5½"
53'-4" TOTAL LENGTH
1 0 FEET 5 10 15 20
13'-0"
7'-3"
4'-0"
6'-4" (ROOF)
7'-4½" (PLATFORMS)
SECTION AT WHISTLE
H.R 134
7'-4½" (PLATFORMS)
6'-1½" (DOORS)
8'-0¾" (RAILS)
7'-2¾" (TANK)
134
VACUUM RESERVOIRS
NO REAR STEPS IN HR DAYS

Plate 96

Plate 97

Plate 96 is of No. 19 when new and fitted with cross tubes, the two covers to the ends being visible on the side of the firebox. Plate 97 shows No. 17699 at Forres in May 1928 still fitted with an original boiler, but modified safety valves on the dome. In plate 98 No. 17703 in the early LMS black livery for goods engines has had the safety valves moved to on top of the firebox.

Plate 98

Plate 99

In another view of a 'Barney' in early LMS days plate 99 depicts No. 17694 at the entrance to Inverness shed in May 1928 coupled to a 3,000 gallon tender.

The common boiler and cylinder design with the 'Small Ben' class led to the same modifications being carried out by the LMS and plate 100 illustrates No. 17704 at Inverness in April 1936, in the modified form.

Plate 100

Plate 101

Plate 102

The logical development of Jones' 'Big Goods' class as an express passenger engine first appeared in 1900, some four years after his resignation. The class was built in three series under the direction of three different Locomotive Engineers and the first under Drummond's supervision are listed below.

In plate 101 No. 144 ***Blair Castle*** was photographed standing at Blair Atholl early this century, while plate 102 illustrates a sister engine No. 146 ***Skibo Castle*** of the second order supplied in 1902 and equipped with Westinghouse brake equipment as well as the usual vacuum brake. Both carry 'HIGHLAND RAILWAY' on the tender sides.

4–6–0 'CASTLE' I CLASS Total 12

HR No.	Builder	Works No.	Built	Name	LMS No.	Withdrawn	Remarks
140	Dübs	3848	6/00	*Taymouth Castle*	14675	8/39	
141	Dübs	3849	6/00	*Ballindalloch Castle*	14676	9/37	Phoenix superheater fitted c '12 to c '16.
142	Dübs	3850	6/00	*Dunrobin Castle*	14677	2/39	
143	Dübs	3851	6/00	*Gordon Castle* (II)	14678	2/46	Extended smokebox fitted in '30. Withdrawn. 6/39, reinstated 9/40.
144	Dübs	3852	6/00	*Blair Castle*	14679	2/36	
145	Dübs	3853	6/00	*Murthly Castle*	14680	5/30	Extended smokebox fitted '26.
146	Dübs	4244	7/02	*Skibo Castle*	14681	10/46	Westinghouse brake, 4,000 gall. tender fitted c '36.
147	Dübs	4245	7/02	*Beaufort Castle*	14682	11/43	Westinghouse brake.
148	Dübs	4246	7/02	*Cawdor Castle*	14683	4/37	Westinghouse brake. Steel fb 6/18 to 1/29.
149	Dübs	4247	7/02	*Duncraig Castle*	14684	1/40	Westinghouse brake.
30	NB Loco	19011	3/10	*Dunvegan Castle*	14685	1/45	
35	NB Loco	19012	2/11	*Urquhart Castle*	14686	7/46	4,000 gallon tender fitted c '37.

Plate 103

Plate 104

Plate 103 depicts No. 144 ***Blair Castle*** in lined Drummond livery and 'THE HIGHLAND RAILWAY' painted on the tender side. Note also the coal well stacked up on the tender. Should a lump fall at the trackside, the surfacemen would be glad of it to warm their bothy in winter time. On the other hand it was not unknown for men to be struck by a piece of coal shaken off an engine or tender.

In plate 104 No. 143 ***Gordon Castle*** (II) is seen after World War I in the plain livery with the later design of number plate and 'H.R' on the tender. The edge of the smokebox, the hinges and dart handle have on the other hand been burnished.

Figure 36 is a drawing of the 'Castle' I class as built.

Figure 36

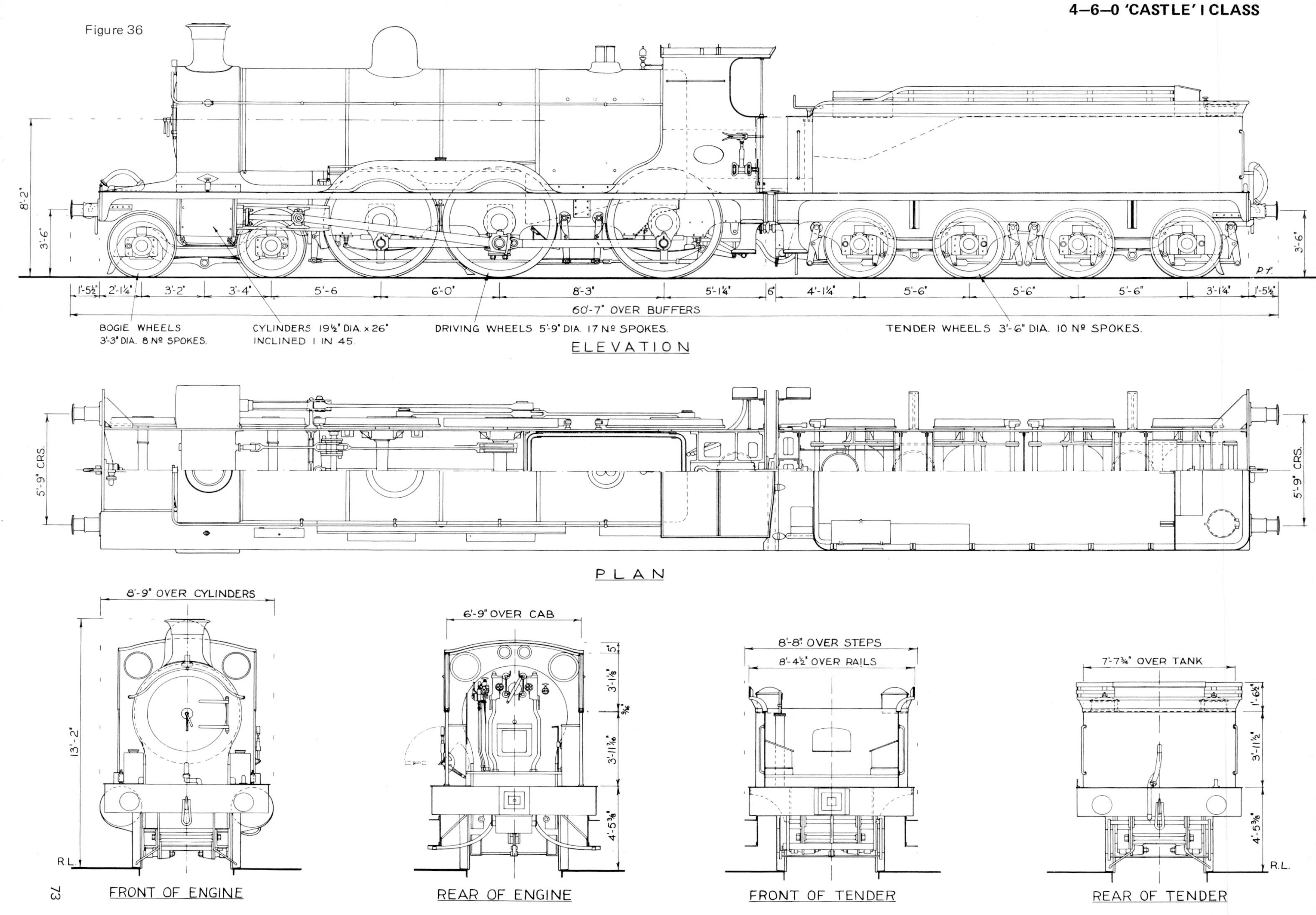
8'-2"
3'-6"
1'-5½"
2'-1¼"
3'-2"
3'-4"
5'-6
6'-0"
8'-3"
5'-1¼"
6"
4'-1¼"
5'-6"
5'-6"
5'-6"
3'-1¼"
1'-5½"
3'-6"
60'-7" OVER BUFFERS
BOGIE WHEELS
3'-3" DIA. 8 Nº SPOKES.
CYLINDERS 19½" DIA. x 26"
INCLINED 1 IN 45.
DRIVING WHEELS 5'-9" DIA. 17 Nº SPOKES.
TENDER WHEELS 3'-6" DIA. 10 Nº SPOKES.
ELEVATION
5'-9" CRS.
5'-9" CRS.
PLAN
8'-9" OVER CYLINDERS
13'-2"
RL
FRONT OF ENGINE
6'-9" OVER CAB
5"
3'-1⅛"
9/16"
3'-11 1/16"
4'-5⅜"
REAR OF ENGINE
8'-8" OVER STEPS
8'-4½" OVER RAILS
FRONT OF TENDER
7'-7¾" OVER TANK
1'-6½"
3'-11½"
4'-5⅜"
R.L.
REAR OF TENDER

Plate 105

Plate 106

For the first seven years of the LMS regime the 'Castles' continued on express passenger work, chiefly between Perth and Inverness and plate 105 shows No. 14678 ***Gordon Castle*** (II) standing outside the Perth shed ready for its turn of duty in May 1930; while No. 14387 ***Loch Garry*** can just be seen on the adjacent road.

Following the introduction of Stanier's 4–6–0 5P5Fs on the Highland lines, the 'Clans' and two 'Castles' were transferred by the LMS to work the Oban line and in plate 106 No. 14686 ***Urquhart Castle*** paired to a 6 wheeled tender makes a departure from Oban. The noise of the engine's exhaust beat will reverberate round the town centre for the next ten minutes as the train is dragged up the 1 in 50 gradient in a great sweep round the town until respite is reached at Glencruitten Crossing.

Plate 107

No. 14680 ***Murthly Castle*** in plate 107 has an extended smokebox similar to the later series. This engine was the first of the class to be withdrawn, but the unusual smokebox feature subsequently appeared on No. 14678 *Gordon Castle* (II).

In plate 108 the view of No. 14677 ***Dunrobin Castle*** demonstrates some of the changes in detail that appeared in the LMS era. As built the 'Castle' I class had marine type 'big ends', but these were in some cases replaced by the solid type. Note also the packing behind the buffer housing, the Caley smokebox door, snap head rivets, and large flat topped dome.

Plate 108

Plate 109

4–6–0 'CASTLE' II CLASS   Total 4

HR No.	Works No.	Built	Name	LMS No.	With-drawn	Remarks
26	20160	4/13	***Brahan Castle***	14687	6/35	
27	20161	7/13	***Thurso Castle***	14688	2/35	
28	20162	7/13	***Cluny Castle***	14689	9/44	Withdrawn 5/39, reinstated 5/41.
43	20163	4/13	***Dalcross Castle***	14690	4/47	4000 gall. tender fitted c '47.

Renumbering:–

43 : 29 5/13

The four 'Castle' class locomotives ordered from the North British Loco Co. during F.G. Smith's tenure of office had minor variations from the previous batches. As may be seen from plate 109 of No. 26 ***Brahan Castle*** in workshop photographic grey livery and the drawing in figure 37 opposite, the most obvious is the extended smokebox, which it has been suggested was intended to allow for a superheater, but if so none was ever fitted to this series. Other differences are longer buffers, the Capuchon chimney, larger dome, solid 'big ends', clipped rectangular front cab windows and coal rails taken to the rear of the tender.

Figure 37

4–6–0 'CASTLE' II CLASS

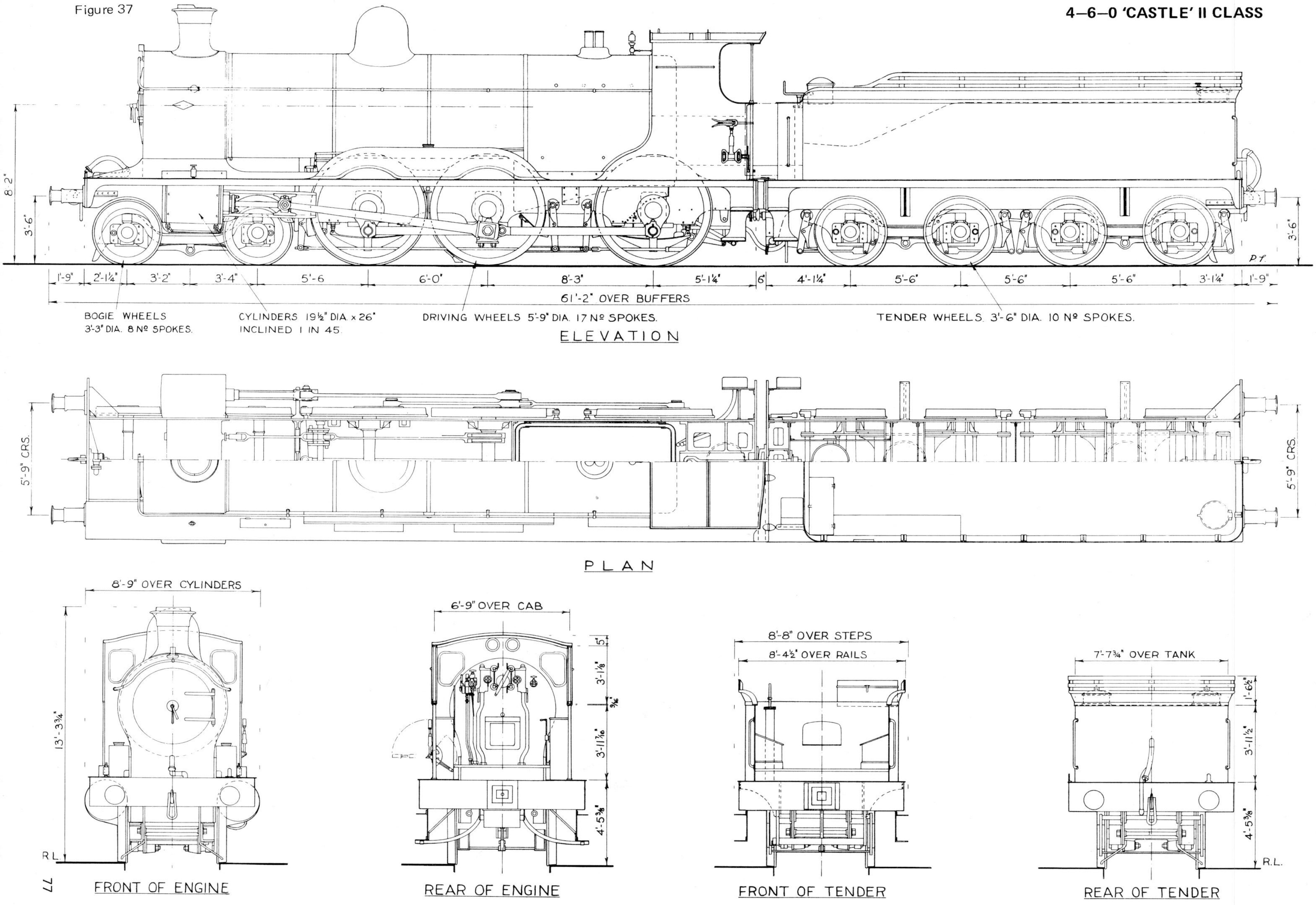

8'-2"
3'-6"
1'-9" 2'-1¼" 3'-2" 3'-4" 5'-6 6'-0" 8'-3" 5'-1¼" 6" 4'-1¼" 5'-6" 5'-6" 5'-6" 3'-1¼" 1'-9"
3'-6"
61'-2" OVER BUFFERS

BOGIE WHEELS
3'-3" DIA. 8 Nº SPOKES.

CYLINDERS 19½" DIA x 26"
INCLINED 1 IN 45

DRIVING WHEELS 5'-9" DIA. 17 Nº SPOKES.

TENDER WHEELS 3'-6" DIA. 10 Nº SPOKES.

ELEVATION

5'-9" CRS.
5'-9" CRS.

PLAN

8'-9" OVER CYLINDERS
13'-3¾"
R.L.

FRONT OF ENGINE

6'-9" OVER CAB
5"
3'-1⅛"
9/16"
3'-11 7/16"
4'-5⅜"

REAR OF ENGINE

8'-8" OVER STEPS
8'-4½" OVER RAILS

FRONT OF TENDER

7'-7¾" OVER TANK
1'-6½"
3'-11½"
4'-5⅜"
R.L.

REAR OF TENDER

Plate 110

Plate 110 depicts ***Brahan Castle*** again, this time in LMS livery and numbered 14687 standing at Wick in July 1931. It carries the unusual feature of a Midland design of smokebox door with dog clip fastenings instead of the more usual dart. The fitting of Ross pop safety valves and ejector pipes outside the boiler on the other hand was common LMS practice. The tender coal rails have also been cut back to in front of the two tank fillers.

Plate 111

In plate 111 No. 14690 ***Dalcross Castle*** is seen leaving Tain with a passenger train in September 1937. The 'Castles' continued to perform excellent work in LMS days being capable of hauling 200 tons unassisted on the steeper Highland gradients or 250 to 300 tons on the easier lengths. Downhill they could run well and had a rapid rate of acceleration on starting.

4–6–0 'CASTLE' III CLASS

The third and last series of three 'Castle' class locomotives were put in hand as a 'stop gap' following the banishment of the 'Rivers'. No doubt with these engines in mind a change from 5 ft 9 in to 6 foot diameter driving wheels was decided upon. This resulted in a slightly longer boiler with higher centre line and altered chimney, dome and cab roof. If, by using an old and well tried design, the idea had been to provide motive power in a hurry, the redesign resulting from this change is likely to have caused delay and as it was this series was never as popular with the enginemen. The 6 wheeled tender on the other hand must be regarded as an improvement.

Plate 112 shows No. 59 *Foulis Castle* when new and figure 38 is a reproduction of the North British Loco Co's diagram.

Plate 112

4–6–0 'CASTLE' III CLASS Total 3

HR No.	Works No.	Built	Name	LMS No.	Withdrawn	Remarks
50	21459	3/17	*Brodie Castle*	14691	9/38	
58	21460	3/17	*Darnaway Castle*	14692	3/46	3,350 gall. tender fitted c '36.
59	21461	4/17	*Foulis Castle*	14693	4/35	

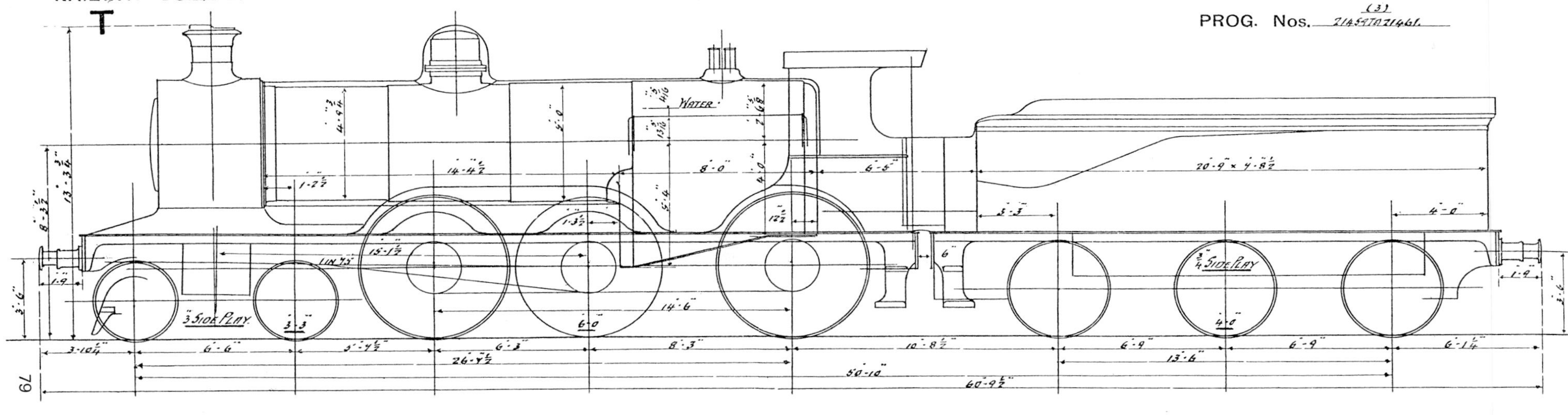

Figure 38

4–6–0 'CASTLE' III CLASS

Plate 113

The two photographs on this page were both taken at the old timber coaling stage Inverness. In plate 113 No. 14693 ***Foulis Castle*** wearing the crimson lake livery is in the process of being coaled in June 1927. Note the wooden coal tubs lined up on the stage.

Probably a few years later No. 14691 ***Brodie Castle*** in plate 114 is facing the opposite way and looking somewhat less well groomed. Whereas the previous two series had been equipped with steam reversers, the final batch had screw reverse and the reach rod is clearly visible in this view. Also because with the increase in driving wheel diameter the connecting rods passed above the running plate, the splashers had to be made wider.

Plate 114

0–6–0T 'SCRAP TANK' CLASS

Plate 115

The Allan locomotives displaced from service by Drummond's new 'Small Ben' and 'Barney' classes led to the scrapping of the older engines and in days before the oxy-acetylene cutting torch the job had to be done the hard way by hand, as shown in plate 115 of the scrap line at Inverness, the Welsh's Bridge signal cabin being behind the 4–4–0 'Jones Tank' in the left background. The availability of three spare replacement boilers for the rebuilt Allan classes led to Lochgorm putting together three powerful 0–6–0 shunting engines, inevitably known as 'Scrap Tanks'. The wheels of course were off the 2–4–0 goods engines and were therefore a little larger than usual for shunting purposes.

Plate 116 illustrates No. 23 of the class at Perth. Note the painted coupling rods and cross-head.

0–6–0T 'SCRAP TANK' CLASS Total 3

HR No.	Built	LMS No.	Withdrawn	Remarks
22	10/03	16380	12/30	Vacuum brake altered to steam 6/20.
23	12/03	16381	12/32	
24	5/04	16382	12/30	Vacuum brake altered to steam 1/13.

Plate 116

0–6–0T 'SCRAP TANK' CLASS

Figure 39

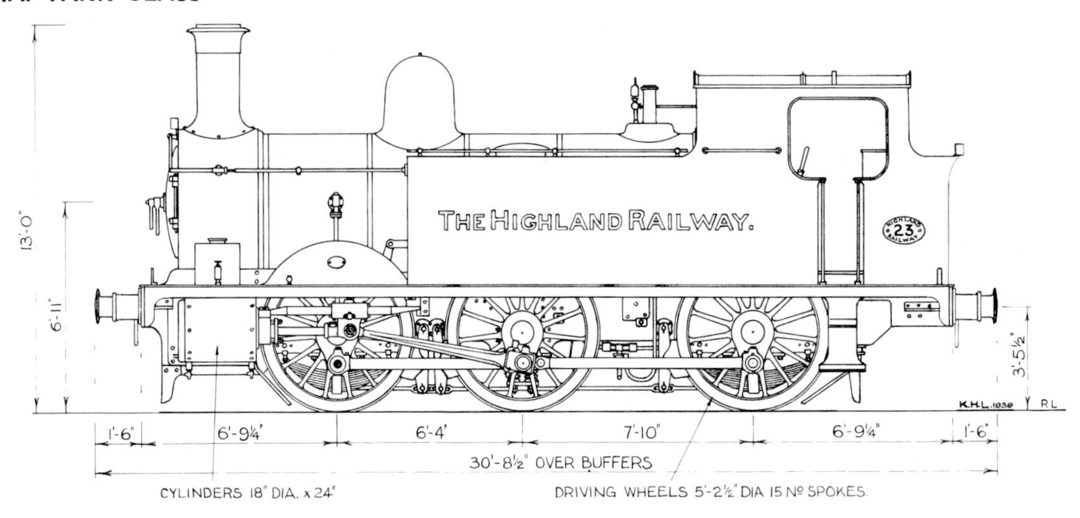

Plate 117

Figure 39 is a drawing for the class prepared from the dimensions detailed and photographs.

Plate 117 taken in May 1928 shows No. 16382 at Perth and plate 118 is of No. 16381 freshly repainted, both being in the LMS early black livery for goods engines. No. 16382 has extension boards to the coal bunker and carries the fire irons on the cab roof.

Plate 118

0–4–4T 'PASSENGER TANK' CLASS

Plate 119

Drummond designed these very neat tank engines for working the various small branches, which were being brought into use at the time. They were the last class of engine constructed at the Company's Lochgorm Works.

Plate 119 shows No. 46 performing the more exotic duty of hauling the Director's saloon on an inspection of the line near Forsinard. Figure 40 is a drawing for the class.

0–4–4T 'PASSENGER TANK' CLASS Total 4

HR No.	Built	Name (if any)	LMS No.	With-drawn	Remarks
25	3/05	*Strathpeffer* (III)	15051	8/56	BR No. 55051.
40	9/05	*Gordon Lennox*	15052	12/30	
45	12/05	–	15053	1/57	BR No. 55053. Last HR engine in service.
46	2/06	–	15054	10/45	

Both named engines had lost their names by 1920.

Figure 40

Plate 120

The class must have looked very fine in crimson lake as first applied by the LMS and plate 120 depicts a spotless No. 15051 at Dingwall in this guise. Note that the vacuum pipe folds sideways to allow the smokebox door to open.

No. 15054 in plate 121 appears a little more 'work-a-day' shunting at Milburn Jct. Inverness in July 1938. The first wagon is an ex North Eastern Rly. 8 ton 3 plank dropside and the second an ex Great Northern 15 ton 8 plank end door coal wagon.

Plate 121

Plate 122

In later years the surviving members of the class were particularly associated with the Dornoch branch, built as a light railway, from The Mound on the main line to the north and the royal burgh of Dornoch. In plate 122 No. 55051 was photographed at the terminus of the head of the branch train in April 1952.

HR Nos 25 and 45 were taken into BR stock as Nos 55051 and 55053, the second becoming the last Highland engine in ordinary service. Plate 123 shows this engine shortly after being painted and fully lined out in BR livery: indeed the lining on the cab and tank fronts, the cab door, wheels, steps and lower sand boxes if not unique is certainly unusual. Withdrawal came rather suddenly when the crank axle broke.

Plate 123

Plate 124

The 'Big Ben' class was very similar to the 'Small Ben' class, but had larger boilers with a slightly higher pressure, although this was later reduced. The first batch were originally supplied with 6 wheeled tenders of 3,185 gallon capacity, whilst the 1909 engines were provided with 8 wheeled tenders of 3,600 gallon capacity and two of the remaining four acquired 3,200 gallon bogie tenders at a later date. The class was intended to work the Inverness-Wick section. The two 'Ben' and 'Barney' classes illustrate admirably the faithful way in which the Highland practice of Peter Drummond followed the South-Western trends of Dugald Drummond; compare the LSWR 'K10', 'S11' and '700' classes.

No. 64 *Ben Mholach*, formerly No. 66, of 'Big Ben' class may be seen in plate 124 in original condition at Blair Atholl. Note the burnished edge to the wing plates and smokebox door seating ring.

4–4–0 'BIG BEN' CLASS Total 6

HR No.	Works No.	Built	Name	Tender when built	Feed water heater Fitted	Feed water heater Removed	LMS No.	Super-heated	With-drawn	Remarks
61	18269	5/08	*Ben na Caillich*	3,185	2/14	11/15	14417	'27	5/36	3,200 gall. tender fitted 12/08.
63	18270	5/08	*Ben Mheadhoin*	3,185	i/s 11/14 o/s 1/15	11/15 8/17	14418	5/24	12/32	3,200 gall. tender fitted 12/08. Steel fb 12/17 to 5/24. Westinghouse brake.
66	18271	5/08	*Ben Mholach*	3,185	i/s 10/13 o/s 5/14	11/15 11/15	14419	'25	10/35	
68	18272	5/08	*Ben a' Chait*	3,185	i/s 11/14 o/s 1/15	11/15 11/16	14420	6/24	4/34	
60	18803	5/09	*Ben Bhreac Mhor*	3,600	2/14	11/15	14421	'24	10/32	Westinghouse brake.
62	18804	5/09	*Ben a' Chaoruinn*	3,600	12/12	4/16	14422	'26	3/37	

Renaming:—

60 : *Ben Bhreac' Mhor* '24

61 : *Ben na Caillach* '26

62 : *Ben Achaoruinn* '26, *Ben a'Chaoruinn*

Renumbering:—

66 : 64 6/09

68 : 65 6/09

Plate 125

Plate 126

Both batches of 'Big Bens' were built by the North British Locomotive combine of Glasgow and in figure 41 their diagram for the second with 3,600 gallon tender is reproduced. F G Smith experimented with both inside and outside feed water heaters and plate 126 shows No. 61 ***Ben na Caillich*** so equipped. This engine, together with Nos 60, 62 and 63, was also fitted with Westinghouse brake gear until about 1917. ***Ben na Caillach*** (mis-spelt) is depicted again in plate 125 resplendent in LMS lined black livery. The bogie tender is of 3,200 gallon capacity and was originally coupled to a 'Barney'.

Figure 41

RAILWAY CO. Highland

GAUGE OF RAILS 4' - 8½"

Plate 127

Plate 127 shows a three quarters view of No. 14420 ***Ben a' Chait*** on a north bound train at Muir of Ord in May 1928. This engine in LMS crimson lake livery has a 6 wheeled 3,185 gallon tender.

Another view of No. 14417 is reproduced in plate 128, illustrating clearly the extended smokebox barrel and new chimney provided as part of the work of superheating these engines. Observe the small additional window in the front of the cab below the usual round spectacle. Presumably the latter were so high that some drivers had difficulty in seeing forward and may account for the modified shape on the second two series of 'Castle' locomotives.

Plate 128

0–6–4T 'BANKING TANK' CLASS

This class was the last introduced to the Highland Railway by Drummond and was designed with banking duties in mind. There were a certain number of design features common to earlier classes, notably the cylinders and wheels from the 'Barneys' and bogie from the 'Castles', to which side tanks and coal bunker were added, thereby producing the heaviest engine on the line to date.

The locomotives were all built by the North British Locomotive Co. under just two orders, the latter being delivered over an extended period of twenty one months. This may have been at the wish of the Highland for financial reasons, two 'Castles' Nos 30 and 35 also being supplied over a period of eleven months in 1910 and '11.

Figure 42 is a drawing for the class and the class list is reproduced below. Some renumbering took place soon after delivery to afford a continuous series for the 'Big Bens', some of which were obtained at the same period and likewise for the 'Castle' II class four years later.

Figure 42

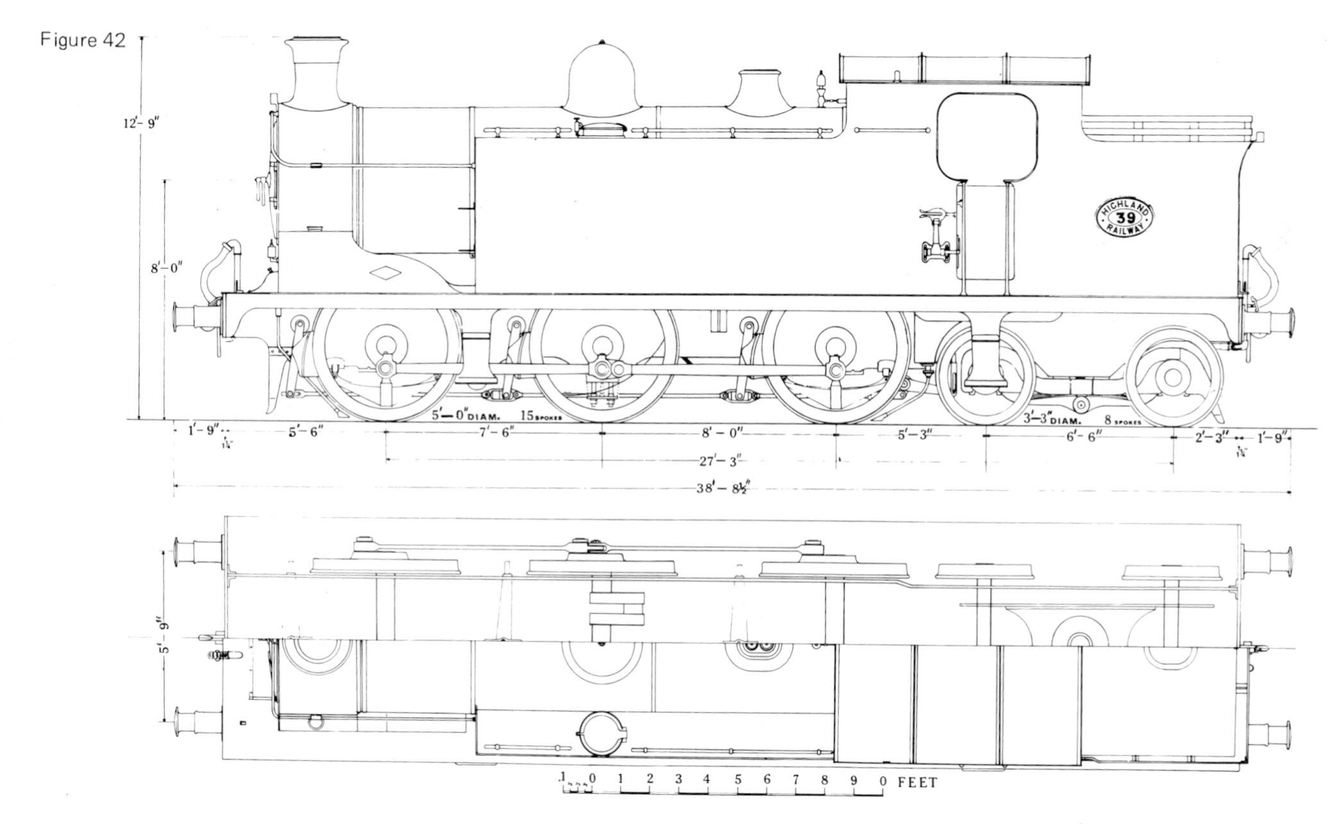

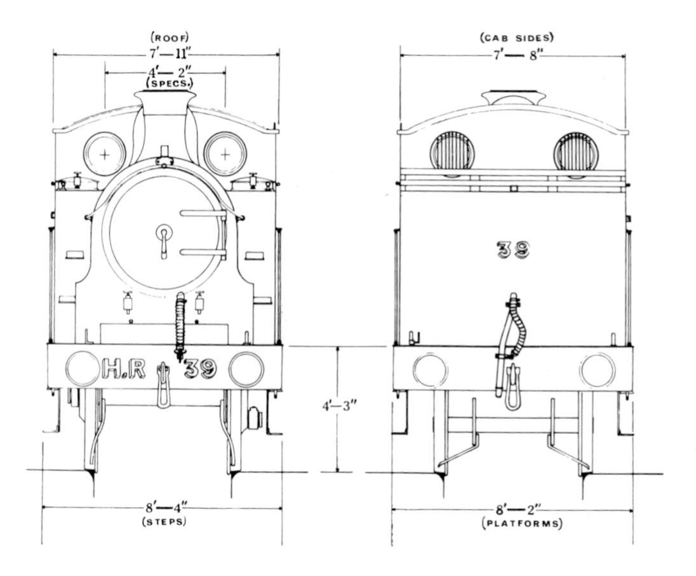

0–6–4T 'BANKING TANK' CLASS — Total 8

HR No.	Works No.	Built	LMS No.	N55/52 boiler carried	With-drawn
39	18805	6/09	15300	11/31	12/36
64	18806	6/09	15301	–	10/34
65	18807	6/09	15302	–	8/33
69	18808	6/09	15303	–	2/32
29	19013	8/10	15304	–	2/32
31	19014	11/11	15305	–	11/34
42	19015	4/12	15306	12/31	11/35
44	19016	4/12	15307	12/31	11/34

Renumbering:–

64 : 66 6/09.
65 : 68 6/09.
29 : 43 5/13.

Plate 129

Plate 130

The handsome appearance of the 'Banking Tanks' can be seen in plate 129 of No. 68 at Blair Atholl, from where the engines were used to assist trains up the 'Hill' to Drumochter 1,484 feet above sea level. Note the tablet exchange apparatus on the right hand side of the engine and facing forward. The fitting of this apparatus to both sides of an engine was unique to this class and in plate 130 of No. 43 at Forres in May 1928 the collecting fork is facing to the rear so that it may be used while the engine is running in reverse. A member of the class was usually allocated to Forres to bank heavy trains up to Dava summit, itself 1,052 feet above sea level.

Surprisingly the class was accorded passenger locomotive status by the LMS and therefore initially some of them were repainted in the attractive crimson lake livery. Plate 131 shows No. 15302 in this style at Inverness in June 1927.

Plate 131

Plate 132

In plate 132 No. 15307 stands outside Blair Atholl shed awaiting the call of duty also in May 1927.

Three engines of the class were reboilered with LMS Northern Division standard boiler N52/55, intended as well for the ex GSWR 0–6–2Ts designed by Drummond following his move to Kilmarnock in 1912. Plate 133 depicts No. 15300 at Blair Atholl in June 1936 carrying such a boiler.

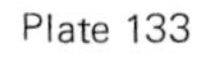

Plate 133

Plate 134

Six of the 'River' class locomotives were ordered from R & W Hawthorn Leslie & Co. of Newcastle-upon-Tyne, but only two were delivered. These engines, although very powerful, proved much too heavy for the Highland line and within a few days of delivery they were withdrawn and sold to the Caledonian Railway, together with the remaining four still in course of construction. Some years later, after track and bridge strengthening had been carried out by the LMS, they returned to perform useful work on the sections for which they were originally intended. There is some doubt about the names proposed for the later engines and these were of course never carried. Design features included Walschaert's valve gear, Robinson superheaters, Belpaire fireboxes, piston valves and a massive 6 wheeled tender.

4–6–0 'RIVER' CLASS   Total 6

HR No.	Works No.	Built	Name	CR No.	LMS No.	Withdrawn
70	3095	9/15	***River Ness***	938	14756	11/39
71	3096	9/15	***River Tay***	939	14757	12/36
(72)	3097	11/15	(*River Beauly*)	940	14758	9/45
(73)	3098	12/15	(*River Spey*)	941	14759	2/39
(74)	3099	12/15	(*River Findhorn*)	942	14760	12/46
(75)	3100	1/16	(*River Garry*)	943	14761	11/39

No. 14760 was originally withdrawn 4/39, but reinstated 9/40.

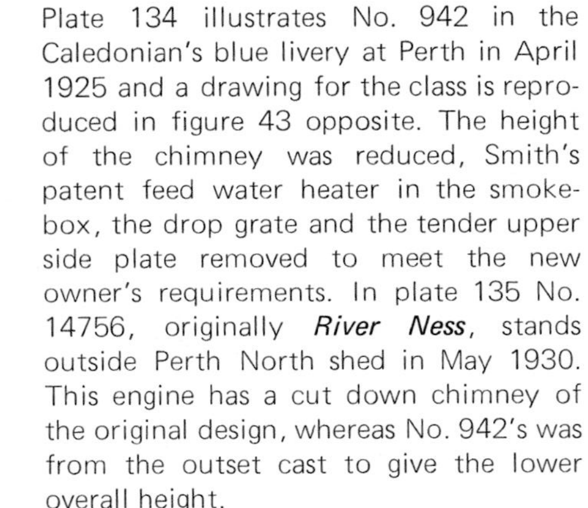

Plate 134 illustrates No. 942 in the Caledonian's blue livery at Perth in April 1925 and a drawing for the class is reproduced in figure 43 opposite. The height of the chimney was reduced, Smith's patent feed water heater in the smokebox, the drop grate and the tender upper side plate removed to meet the new owner's requirements. In plate 135 No. 14756, originally ***River Ness***, stands outside Perth North shed in May 1930. This engine has a cut down chimney of the original design, whereas No. 942's was from the outset cast to give the lower overall height.

Plate 135

Figure 43

4–6–0 'RIVER' CLASS

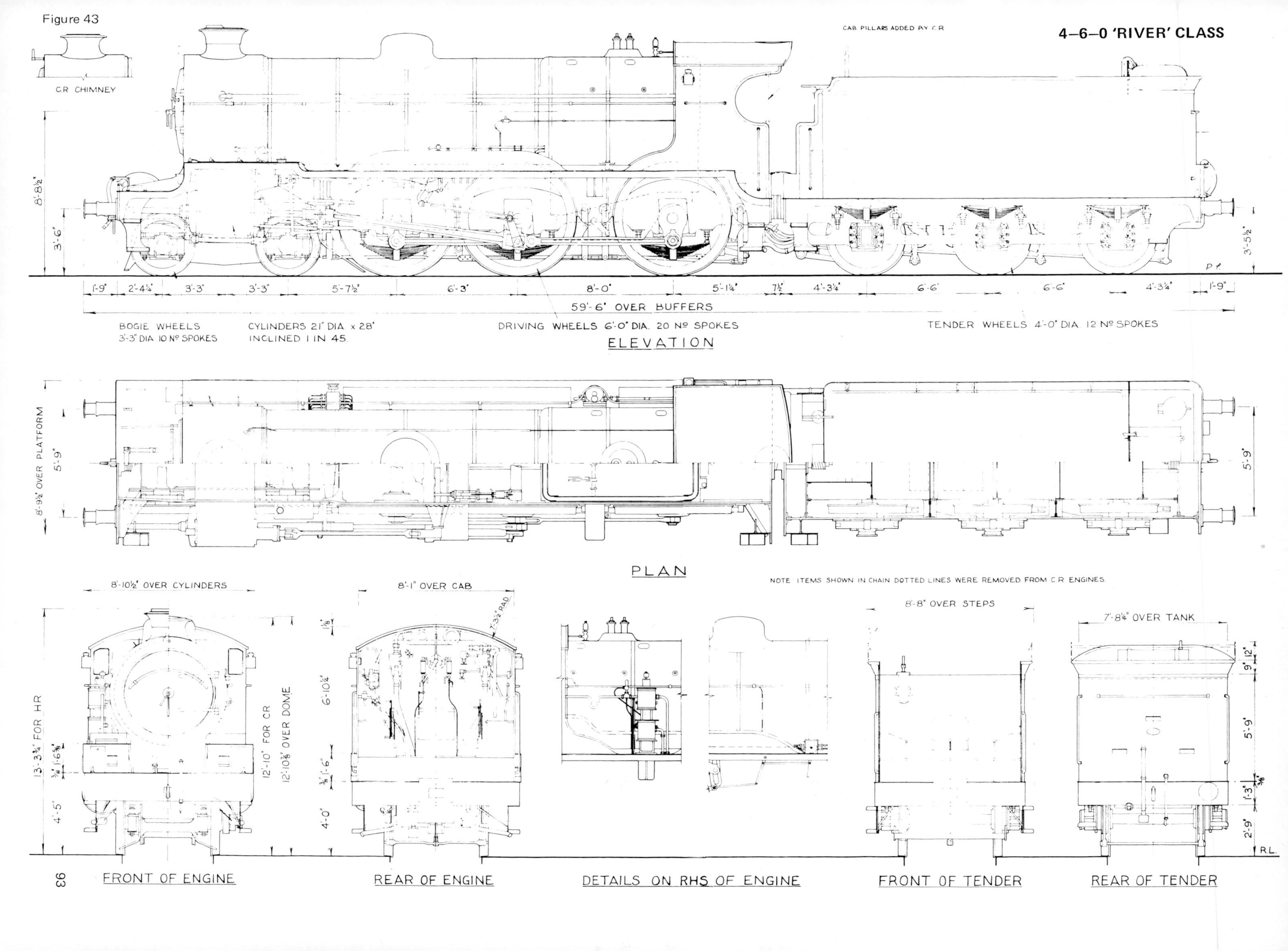

Plate 136

The two members of the 'No. 73' class built by Hawthorn Leslie were powerful passenger engines embodying such refinements as outside mounted Walschaert's valve gear, Robinson superheaters, Belpaire fireboxes, Ross 'pop' safety valves and Wakefield mechanical lubricators as illustrated in figure 44 opposite. They were intended to work the mail trains to Wick and plate 136 shows No. 74 ***Durn*** (II) on the turntable there in March 1924. Note the serif style of number on the plate and the full coat of arms on the splasher below the name. When the engines were new only the garter was applied.

In plate 137 No. 14522 ***Snaigow*** is seen with a Perth bound train at Blair Atholl. Apart from the obvious change in livery, notice that the cabside lamp has been removed and plated up.

4–4–0 'No. 73' CLASS Total 2

HR No.	Works No.	Built	Name	LMS No.	Withdrawn
73	3172	11/16	***Snaigow***	14522	4/36
74	3173	11/16	***Durn*** (II)	14523	4/35

Plate 137

Figure 44

4–4–0 'No. 73' CLASS

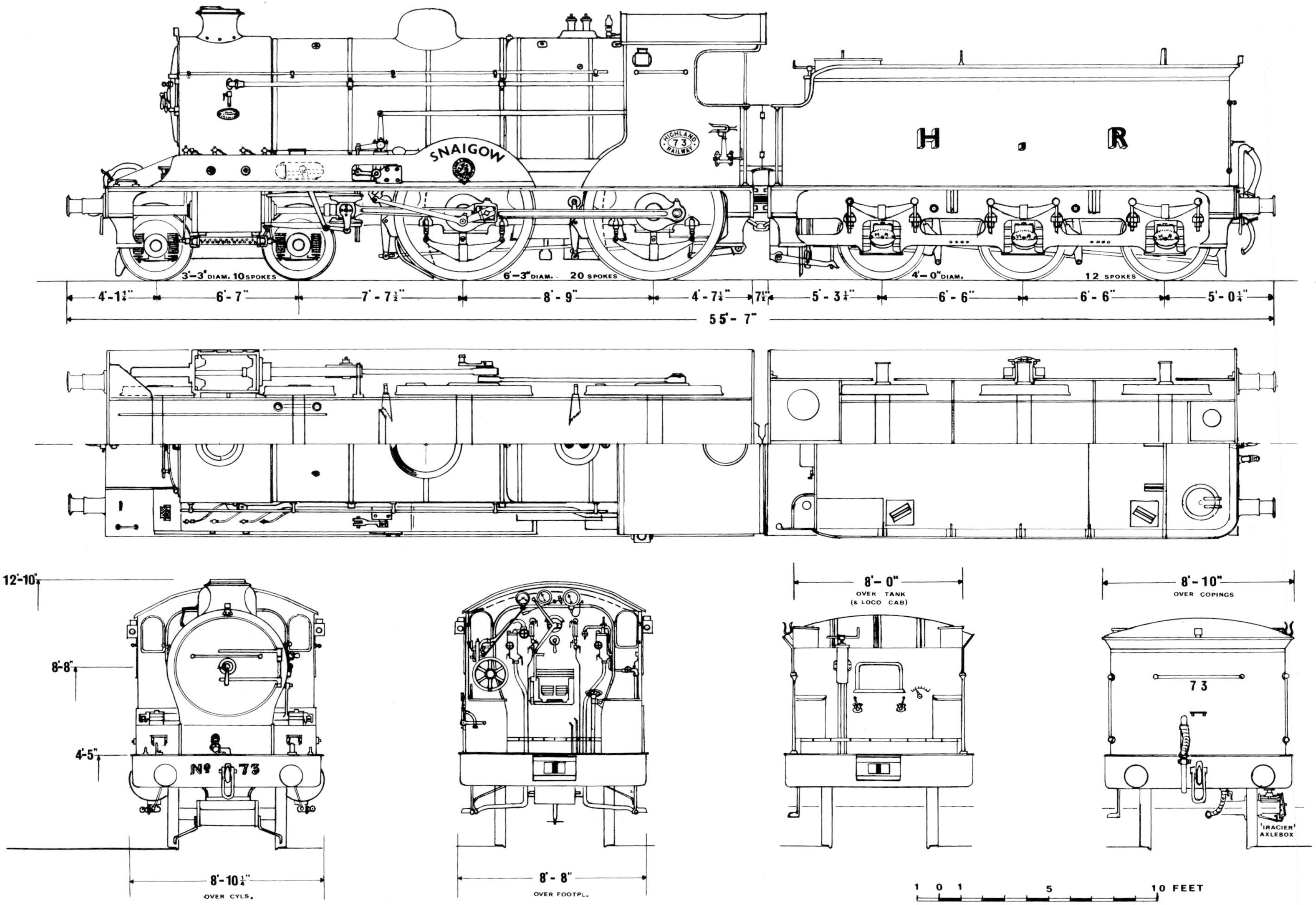

3'–3" DIAM. 10 SPOKES
6'–3" DIAM. 20 SPOKES
4'–0" DIAM.
12 SPOKES
4'-1¼" 6'-7" 7'-7½" 8'-9" 4'-7¼" 7½" 5'-3¼" 6'-6" 6'-6" 5'-0¼"
55'-7"
SNAIGOW
HIGHLAND 73 RAILWAY
H . R
12'-10"
8'-8"
4'-5"
Nº 73
8'-10¼" OVER CYLS.
8'-8" OVER FOOTPL.
8'-0" OVER TANK (& LOCO CAB)
8'-10" OVER COPINGS
73
'IRACIER' AXLEBOX
1 0 1 5 10 FEET

Plate 138

4–6–0 'SUPERHEATED GOODS' CLASS Total 8

HR No.	Works No.	Built	Steel fb removed	LMS No.	BR No.	With-drawn
75	3286	4/18	u/k	17950	57950	8/50
76	3287	4/18	6/22	17951	57951	5/51
77	3288	5/18	'24	17952	–	10/46
78	3289	6/18	'23	17953	(57953)	10/48
79	3371	10/19	–	17954	57954	10/52
80	3372	10/19	–	17955	57955	6/52
81	3373	10/19	–	17956	57956	5/52
82	3374	10/19	–	17957	–	3/46

Durn by now renumbered 14523 by the LMS appears again in plate 138, at Aviemore in June 1928. With only two in the class and reputedly rough riders, they soon fell victim to the LMS standardisation programme and were withdrawn by 1936.

Following the 'No. 73' class, an updated version of Jones' 4–6–0 'Big Goods' class appeared from the Hawthorn Leslie stable incorporating all the refinements of the previous 4–4–0 design. Known officially as the 'Superheated Goods', in view of the obvious similarities to the 4–6–0 'Clan' class about to be described, enthusiasts called them the 'Clan Goods', despite the fact that they preceded the 'Clans'. Built in two batches the first four were provided with lever operated reversing gear, whilst a change was made to screw reverse on the second four with the reach rod clearly visible on the left hand side. Due to the severe shortage of copper at the time of their construction the first four also had steel fireboxes, but in the days before such things could be welded, their life was not long and at the first opportunity they were replaced by the conventional copper type.

In plate 139 No. 80 is seen slung from an overhead crane in Hawthorn Leslie's erection shop in 1919, while another engine of the class in a less advanced stage of construction is below.

Plate 139

4–6–0 'SUPERHEATED GOODS' CLASS

Plate 140

Plates 140 and 141 both show No. 78 of the first batch at Inverness in Highland livery and still equipped with the cabside lamp and Robinson cylinder drain cocks in August 1925, but the standard arrangement of lamp irons has already been fitted by the LMS.

Plate 141

All vacuum brake fitted engines built or rebuilt during Jones' regime, except the 'Yankee Tanks', 'No. 17' and 'No. 13' classes, had front pipes that folded usually in the backward direction thereby permitting the snowploughs to be mounted, although the rebuilt 2–4–0s and 'Jones Tanks' laid sideways. On the other hand, all Drummond engines, except the 'Castles' and 'Passenger Tanks', had fixed pipes, but with the 'River' and subsequent classes backward folding pipes were reintroduced, as shown in these photographs.

Every class of locomotive designed during Cumming's tenure of office had tenders mounted on 'Iracier' patent axle boxes and a close up of the cover to this, the horn block and springing is depicted in plate 142 of No. 57956 at Kyle in April 1952.

A drawing for this class with variations is reproduced in figure 45 overleaf.

Plate 142

Figure 45

4–6–0 'SUPERHEATED GOODS' CLASS

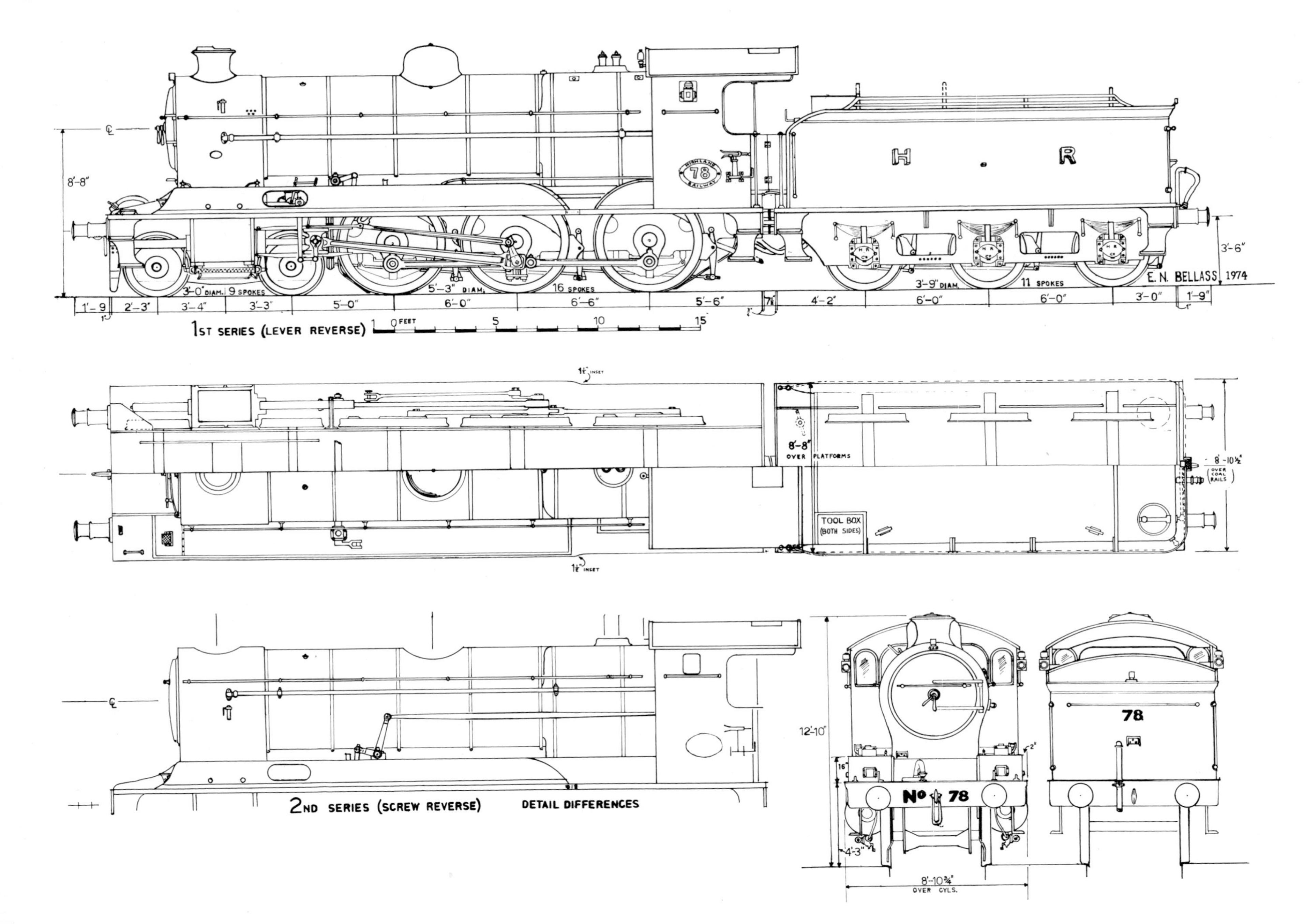

Plate 143

Plate 143 illustrates No. 17951 at Perth in the earlier LMS style of black livery with the large numbers on the tender. The design was very compact, which enabled them to be turned on 50 foot turntables.

Plate 144

In later years the 'Superheaters' were best known for their work on the Kyle line, which they virtually made their own from 1928 until the late forties, aided to a lesser extent by the remaining 'Big Goods' and 'Small Bens'. In plate 144 No. 17953 stands at the entrance to Kyle shed in June 1937.

Plate 145

In plate 145 No. 17950 has just arrived at Inverness with a train from Kyle in September 1937. Note the Caley chimney and smokebox door handle, the two steps on the front of the smokebox itself and the small opening cut in the splasher above the leading driving wheel to ease the task of oiling the valve gear.

All but two members of the class survived to be nationalised, but with the renewal of the turntable at Kyle in 1946 and the subsequent passing of the Skye line for Stanier 5P5Fs, their days were numbered and plate 146 shows the last, No. 57954, in BR livery shortly before withdrawal. Note the Caley snifting valve mounted on the smokebox behind the chimney and the LMS drain cocks.

Plate 146

Plate 147

Plate 148

The final class of engines were the 'Clans' supplied by Hawthorn Leslie to two orders in 1919 and 1921. In plate 147 No. 51 ***Clan Fraser*** of the first batch is in original condition and the company's coat of arms on the rear of the deep casing above the footplate, the drum type smokebox mounted on a saddle casting and the painted flutes to the coupling rods should be observed. Plate 148 shows No. 56 ***Clan Mackenzie*** of the later batch at Perth with a young lad sitting on the running plate.

Plate 149

Plate 149 is a rare view of No. 53 ***Clan Stewart*** at Blair Atholl while equipped with Scarab oil fuel apparatus between January and November 1921, as the five 100 gallon oil tanks on the tender clearly testify. The provision of this equipment is sometimes attributed to the coal strike that year, but in fact coal had been in short supply for some time before and the strike did not commence until near the end of the experiment. It was more likely a genuine attempt to find long term economy in fuel costs.

Plate 150

The 'Clan' class was the last of a long line of locomotives built for the Highland Railway, where the ability to haul often heavy trains up and safely retard them on their way down grades unequalled elsewhere in the country, along single lines, sometimes in extreme weather conditions, or economically operate an infrequent branch line service counted for more than speed and mere thermal efficiency. The 'Clans' were a powerful class of passenger engine intended principally for working the heavy trains between Perth and Inverness. Three and a half years after the despatch of the 'Rivers', the 'Clans' achieved the original performance specification by use of a smaller boiler pressed to a higher pressure, shorter stroke cylinders and a saving in weight of 15 tons. Had they been available in 1915, how different the Highland's problems might have been.

Like the 'Rivers' however, Walschaert's valve gear, 10 inch diameter piston valves, cylinder tail rods, the Robinson superheater, a Belpaire firebox and the Wakefield mechanical lubricator were among features of the class. As with the 'Superheated Goods' class the first four were fitted with steel fireboxes, which did not last too long. All driving wheels had flanges, but these were thinner than previously used.

In plate 150 No. 56 ***Clan Mackenzie*** of the 1921 order is seen when new. There were several minor differences between the two batches as illustrated in figure 46 reproduced opposite, to which must be added the number of changes carried out during the working lives of the engines. All had Westinghouse brakes at some time, but not necessarily when new or after the mid '30s.

4–6–0 'CLAN' CLASS Total 8

HR No.	Works No.	Built	Name	LMS No.	Steel fb removed	Withdrawn
49	3329	4/19	*Clan Campbell*	14762	'24	6/47
51	3330	4/19	*Clan Fraser*	14763	'23	8/44
52	3331	4/19	*Clan Munro*	14764	'24	2/48
53	3332	6/19	*Clan Stewart*	14765	'23	2/45
54	3443	7/21	*Clan Chattan*	14766	–	4/44
55	3444	7/21	*Clan Mackinnon*	14767	–	2/50
56	3445	7/21	*Clan Mackenzie*	14768	–	3/45
57	3446	8/21	*Clan Cameron*	14769	–	10/43

Only No. 55 was allocated a BR number – 54767.

Figure 46

4–6–0 'CLAN' CLASS

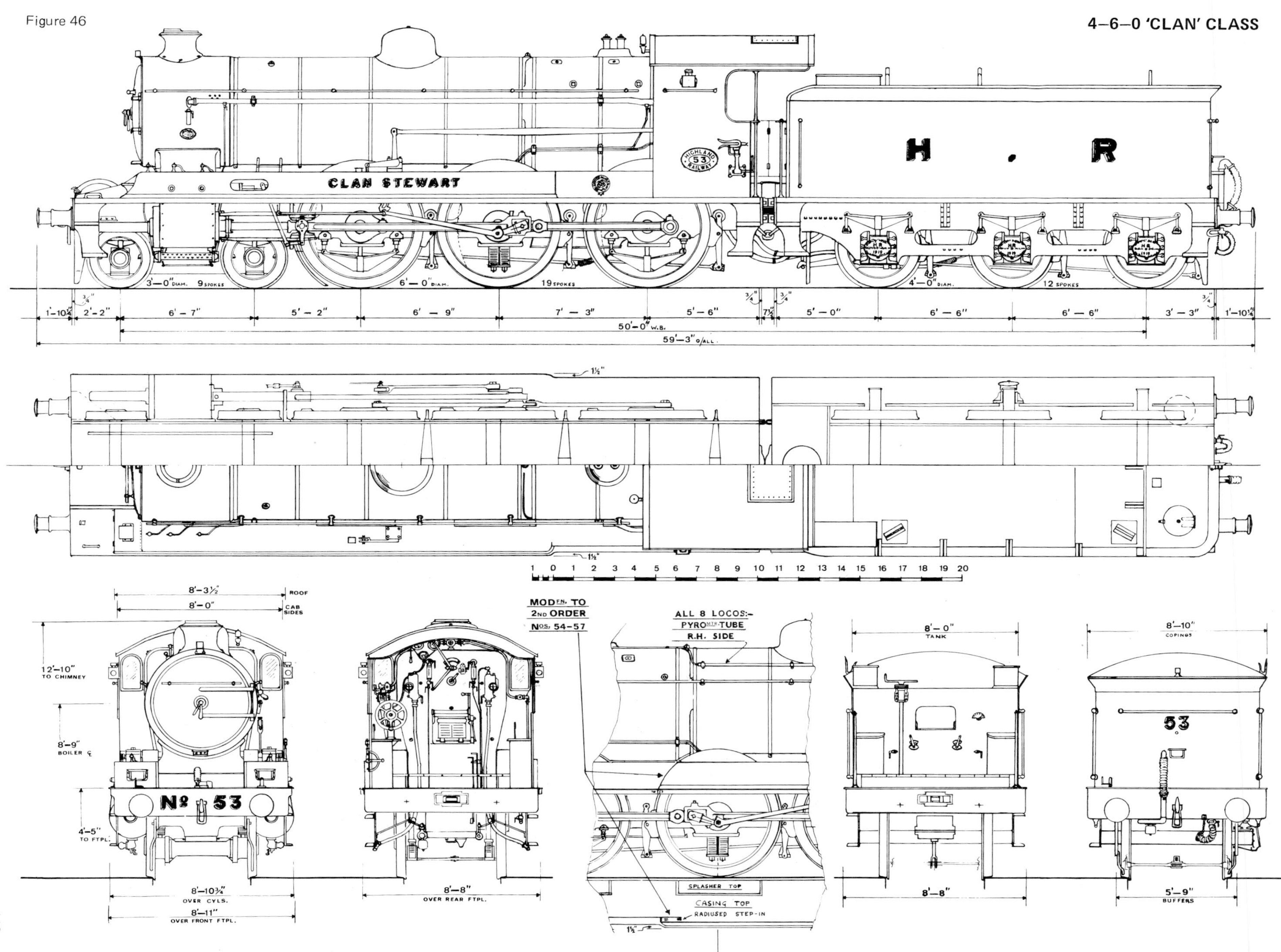

Plate 151

Plate 152

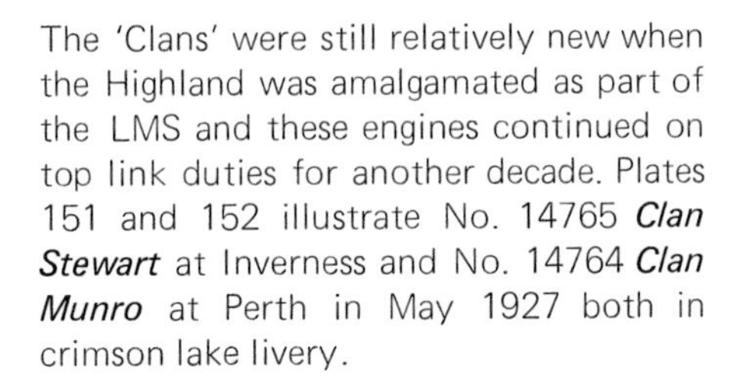

The 'Clans' were still relatively new when the Highland was amalgamated as part of the LMS and these engines continued on top link duties for another decade. Plates 151 and 152 illustrate No. 14765 ***Clan Stewart*** at Inverness and No. 14764 ***Clan Munro*** at Perth in May 1927 both in crimson lake livery.

As mentioned earlier, in 1934 the whole class, together with two 'Castle' locomotives were transferred to work the Callander and Oban section, where improved motive power was urgently required. Plate 153 shows No. 14765 ***Clan Stewart***, this time in the later lined black livery, at Stirling in June 1937.

Plate 153

Plate 154

Still in service on the Highland Section is No. 14769 *Clan Cameron* in plate 154 seen on the turntable at Inverness in May 1930.

After World War II the few remaining members of the class returned to their home ground and were permitted from 1939 to work to Kyle. One, *Clan Mackinnon*, achieved a BR number, 54767, and the final day of reckoning came early in 1950, plate 155 catching the engine at St. Rollox on 4th February on its way to Kilmarnock for scrapping.

Plate 155

Many readers will recall the swan song of the Highland locomotive when during the early '60s the preserved Jones 'Big Goods' gave pleasure to many by hauling specially chartered trains, appearing on television in the ***Railway Roundabout*** series, while providing the motive power on the regular service trains to Kyle of Lochalsh, and finally in the film ***Those Magnificent Men and their Flying Machines***. In plates 156 and 157 No. 103 is seen steaming out from Tain for the last time with the SLS/RCTS Scottish Rail Tour on 15th June 1962. The engine is at the time of writing a static exhibit in the Glasgow Museum of Transport, from where it is to be hoped she may be allowed to emerge once again.

Plate 156

Plate 157

BIBLIOGRAPHY

Ahrons, E L, ***Locomotive and train working in the later part of the nineteenth century,*** Vol. 3, W Heffer, Cambridge, 1952.

Allan, A, numerous papers, ***Proceedings of the Institution of Mechanical Engineers,*** 1853 to 1862.

Atkins, C P, ***Scottish 4–6–0 classes,*** Ian Allan, 1976.

Binney, C, ***Brighton Terriers,*** Ravensbourne Press.

Campbell Cornwell, H J, ***William Stroudley – craftsman of steam,*** David & Charles, Newton Abbot, 1968.

Le Chatelier, M L, translated Gordon, L D B, ***Railway economy,*** Edmonston & Douglas, Edinburgh, 1869.

Ellis, C H, ***Highland engines and their work,*** Locomotive Publishing Co., 1930.

Essery, R J, and Jenkinson, D, ***Locomotive liveries of the LMS,*** Roundhouse/Ian Allan, 1967.

Highet, C, ***Scottish locomotive history 1831-1923,*** George Allen & Unwin, 1970.

Lambert, A J, ***Highland Railway Album*** Vols. 1 and 2 Ian Allan, 1974 and 1978.

Lemon, E J H, ***Pioneer work in locomotive standardisation, construction, maintenance and repair aspects of a historic type – the 'Jones Goods' 4–6–0s Highland Railway,*** a paper thought to have been read to a professional or railway institution, circa 1936/7.

Mitchell, J, ***Reminiscences of my life in the Highlands,*** Vol. 2, David & Charles reprint, Newton Abbot, 1971.

Nock, O S, ***The Highland Railway,*** Ian Allan, 1965.

Reed, B, ***Jones Goods and Indian L,*** Profile No. 17, Windsor, 1971.

Scrutator, ***Behind the Highland Engines***, Inverness, 1913.

Stuart, D H, and Reed, B, ***The Crewe type*** Profile No. 15, Windsor, 1971.

Vallance, H A, ***The Highland Railway,*** MacDonald, 1938, revised David & Charles, Dawlish, 1963.

The Highland Railway Company and its constituents and successors 1855-1955, Stephenson Locomotive Society, 1955.

Various issues of:–
The Engineer, Engineering, Journal of the Stephenson Locomotive Society, Locomotive Magazine, Model Railway Constructor, Model Railways, Model Railway News, Railway Club Journal, The Railway Engineer, Railway Magazine, Railway Modeller, Railway Observer, Railway World, Transport and Railroad Gazette, Trains Illustrated.

The pair of 4–4–0 'Lochs' at Perth shortly before World War I are No. 127 *Loch Garry* and No. 131 *Loch Shin* with extended tender.

P. Tatlow collection

108

APPENDIX 1

APPENDIX 1

LOCOMOTIVES OF THE HIGHLAND RAILWAY, 1865

No.	Type	Builder	Works No.	Building Date	Name	Withdrawal Date
1	2–2–2	Hawthorns (Leith)	(129)	1855	Raigmore	1873
2	2–2–2	"	(130)	1855	Aldourie	1871
3	2–2–2	"	(146)	1856	St. Martin's	1869
4	2–2–2	"	(161)	1857	Ardross	1870
5	2–4–0	"	(163)	1858	Seafield	1897
6	2–4–0	"	(164)	1858	Bruce	1893
7	2–4–0	"	(165)	1858	Fife	1899
8	2–4–0	"	(175)	1858	Altyre	1893
9	2–4–0	"	(176)	1858	—	1893
10	2–4–0	"	(177)	1858	—	1897
11	2–4–0	"	(209)	1859	Skibo	1897
12	2–2–2	"	(258)	1862	—	1898
13	2–2–2	"	(259)	1862	—	1890
14	2–4–0	"	(264)	1862	—	1901
15	2–4–0	"	(265)	1862	—	1893
16	0–4–0T	Neilson	(422)	1859	—	1872
17	0–4–0T	Hawthorns (Leith)	(275)	1863	—	1902
18	2–4–0	Sharp Stewart	(1416)	1863	—	1906
19	2–4–0	"	(1417)	1863	—	1896
20	2–4–0	"	(1426)	1863	—	1906
21	2–4–0	"	(1427)	1863	—	1909
22	2–4–0	"	(1436)	1863	—	1896
23	2–4–0	"	(1437)	1863	—	1902
24	2–4–0	"	(1438)	1863	—	1904
25	2–4–0	"	(1439)	1863	—	1905
26	2–4–0	"	(1440)	1863	—	1896
27	2–4–0	"	(1441)	1863	—	1923
28	2–2–2	Hawthorns (Leith)	(299)	1863	Glenbarry	1898
29	2–2–2	"	(300)	1863	Highlander	1898
30	2–2–2	Neilson	(966)	1863	Prince	1893
31	2–2–2	"	(967)	1863	Princess	1898
32	2–2–2	"	(968)	1863	Sutherland	1898
33	2–2–2	"	(969)	1863	Atholl	1898
34	2–2–2	"	(970)	1863	Seafields	1897
35	2–2–2	"	(971)	1863	Kingsmills	1923
36	2–4–0	Sharp Stewart	(1506)	1864	—	1902
37	2–4–0	"	(1507)	1864	—	1915
38	2–4–0	"	(1508)	1864	—	1902
39	2–4–0	"	(1509)	1864	—	1902
40	2–4–0	"	(1510)	1864	—	1905
41	2–4–0	"	(1511)	1864	—	1906
42	2–4–0	"	(1512)	1864	—	1923
43	2–4–0	"	(1513)	1864	—	1898
44	2–4–0	"	(1519)	1864	—	1912
45	2–4–0	"	(1520)	1864	—	1905
46	2–2–2	Neilson	(1055)	1864	Clachnacuddin	1906
47	2–2–2	"	(1057)	1864	Lovat	1906
48	2–2–2	"	(1056)	1864	Cadboll	1892
49	2–2–2	"	(1058)	1864	Belladrum	1899
50	2–2–2	"	(1059)	1864	Aultnaskiah	1897
51	2–2–2	"	(1054)	1864	Caithness	1893
52	2–2–2	"	(1060)	1864	Dunphail	1899
53	2–2–2	"	(1061)	1864	Stafford	1893
54	2–2–2	"	(1062)	1864	Macduff	1898
55	2–2–2	"	(1063)	1864	Cluny	1906

APPENDIX 2

APPENDIX 2

LOCOMOTIVES OF THE HIGHLAND RAILWAY, 1922

No.	Type	Builder	Works No.	Building Date	Name	LMS No.
1	4–4–0	Dubs	(3685)	1898	Ben-y-Gloe	14397
2	4–4–0	"	(3686)	1898	Ben Alder	14398
3	4–4–0	"	(3687)	1898	Ben Wyvis	14399
4	4–4–0	"	(3688)	1899	Ben More	14400
5	4–4–0	"	(3689)	1899	Ben Vrackie	14401
6	4–4–0	"	(3690)	1899	Ben Armin	14402
7	4–4–0	"	(3691)	1899	Ben Attow	14403
8	4–4–0	"	(3692)	1899	Ben Clebrig	14404
9	4–4–0	Lochgorm	—	1899	Ben Rinnes	14405
10	4–4–0	"	—	1899	Ben Slioch	14406
11	4–4–0	"	—	1899	Ben Macdhui	14407
12	4–4–0	"	—	1900	Ben Hope	14408
13	4–4–0	"	—	1900	Ben Alisky	14409
14	4–4–0	"	—	1900	Ben Dearg	14410
15	4–4–0	"	—	1901	Ben Loyal	14411
16	4–4–0	"	—	1901	Ben Avon	14412
17	4–4–0	"	—	1901	Ben Alligan	14413
18	0–6–0	Dubs	(4240)	1902	—	17699
19	0–6–0	"	(4241)	1902	—	17700
20	0–6–0	"	(4242)	1902	—	17701
21	0–6–0	"	(4243)	1902	—	17702
22	0–6–0T	Lochgorm	—	1903	—	16380
23	0–6–0T	"	—	1903	—	16381
24	0–6–0T	"	—	1904	—	16382
25	0–4–4T	"	—	1905	—	15051
26	4–6–0	N.B. Loco. Co.	(20160)	1913	Brahan Castle	14687
27	4–6–0	"	(20161)	1913	Thurso Castle	14688
27A	2–4–0	Sharp Stewart	(1441)	1863	—	—
28	4–6–0	N.B. Loco. Co.	(20162)	1913	Cluny Castle	14689
29	4–6–0	"	(20163)	1913	Dalcross Castle	14690
30	4–6–0	"	(19011)	1910	Dunvegan Castle	14685
31	0–6–4T	"	(19014)	1911	—	15305
32	4–4–0	Lochgorm	—	1897	—	14282
33	4–4–0	"	—	1897	—	14283
34	4–4–0	"	—	1898	—	14284
35	4–6–0	N.B. Loco. Co.	(19012)	1911	Urquhart Castle	14686
35A	2–4–0	Neilson	(971)	1863	Isla Bank	—
36	0–6–0	N.B. Loco. Co.	(17896)	1907	—	17703
37	0–6–0	"	(17897)	1907	—	17704
37A	2–4–0	Sharp Stewart	(1512)	1864	—	—
38	4–4–0	N.B. Loco. Co.	(17398)	1906	Ben Udlaman	14414
39	0–6–4T	"	(18805)	1909	—	15300
40	0–4–4T	Lochgorm	—	1905	—	15052
41	4–4–0	N.B. Loco. Co.	(17399)	1906	Ben Bhach Ard	14415
42	0–6–4T	"	(19015)	1912	—	15306
43	0–6–4T	"	(19013)	1910	—	15304
44	0–6–4T	"	(19016)	1912	—	15307
45	0–4–4T	Lochgorm	—	1905	—	15053
46	0–4–4T	"	—	1906	—	15054
47	4–4–0	N.B. Loco. Co.	(17400)	1906	Ben a'Bhuird	14416
48	4–4–0	Lochgorm	—	1901	—	14285
49	4–6–0	Hawthorn Leslie	(3329)	1919	Clan Campbell	14762
49A	0–6–0T	Lochgorm	—	1874	Fort George	16383
50	4–6–0	N.B. Loco. Co.	(21459)	1917	Brodie Castle	14691
50B	4–4–0T	Lochgorm	—	1879	—	15012
51	4–6–0	Hawthorn Leslie	(3330)	1919	Clan Fraser	14763
51B	4–4–0T	Dubs	(3077)	1893	—	(15015)
52	4–6–0	Hawthorn Leslie	(3331)	1919	Clan Munro	14764
52B	4–4–0T	Dubs	(3079)	1893	—	15016

Appendix 2 – Locomotives of the Highland Railway, 1922 – Continued

No.	Type	Builder	Works No.	Building Date	Name	LMS No.
53	4–6–0	Hawthorn Leslie	(3332)	1919	Clan Stewart	14765
53A	0–4–4T	Lochgorm	—	1890	Lybster	15050
54	4–6–0	Hawthorn Leslie	(3443)	1921	Clan Chattan	14766
54B	4–4–0T	Dubs	(3078)	1893	—	15017
55	4–6–0	Hawthorn Leslie	(3444)	1921	Clan Mackinnon	14767
56	4–6–0	"	(3445)	1921	Clan Mackenzie	14768
56B	0–6–0T	Lochgorm	—	1869	Dornoch	16118
57	4–6–0	Hawthorn Leslie	(3446)	1921	Clan Cameron	14769
57B	0–6–0T	Lochgorm	—	1872	—	16119
58	4–6–0	N.B. Loco. Co.	(21460)	1917	Darnaway Castle	14692
58B	4–4–0T	Lochgorm	—	1878	—	15011
59	4–6–0	N.B. Loco. Co.	(21461)	1917	Foulis Castle	14693
59B	4–4–0T	Lochgorm	—	1879	—	15010
60	4–4–0	N.B. Loco. Co.	(18803)	1909	Ben Bhreac Mhor	14421
61	4–4–0	"	(18269)	1908	Ben na Caillich	14417
62	4–4–0	"	(18804)	1909	Ben a'Chaoruinn	14422
63	4–4–0	"	(18270)	1908	Ben Mheadhouin	14418
64	4–4–0	"	(18271)	1908	Ben Mholach	14419
65	4–4–0	"	(18272)	1908	Ben a'Chait	14420
66	0–6–4T	"	(18806)	1909	—	15301
67	4–4–0	Dubs	(721)	1874	Cromartie	—
68	0–6–4T	N.B. Loco. Co.	(18807)	1909	—	15302
69	0–6–4T	"	(18809)	1909	—	15303
70	4–4–0	"	(21456)	1917	Loch Ashie	14394
70A	4–4–0	Lochgorm	—	1882	—	14277
71	4–4–0	N.B. Loco. Co.	(21457)	1917	Loch Garve	14395
72	4–4–0	"	(21458)	1917	Loch Ruthven	14396
72A	4–4–0	Lochgorm	—	1884	Grange	—
73	4–4–0	Hawthorn Leslie	(3172)	1916	Snaigow	14522
73A	4–4–0	Lochgorm	—	1885	Rosehaugh	—
74	4–4–0	Hawthorn Leslie	(3173)	1916	Durn	14523
75	4–6–0	"	(3286)	1918	—	17950
75A	4–4–0	Lochgorm	—	1886	Breadalbane	—
76	4–6–0	Hawthorn Leslie	(3287)	1918	—	17951
76A	4–4–0	Clyde Loco. Co.	(1)	1886	Bruce	—
77	4–6–0	Hawthorn Leslie	(3288)	1918	—	17952
77A	4–4–0	Clyde Loco. Co.	(2)	1886	Lovat	—
78	4–6–0	Hawthorn Leslie	(3289)	1918	—	17953
78A	4–4–0	Clyde Loco. Co.	(3)	1886	Lochalsh	—
79	4–6–0	Hawthorn Leslie	(3371)	1919	—	17954
79A	4–4–0	Clyde Loco. Co.	(4)	1886	Atholl	—
80	4–6–0	Hawthorn Leslie	(3372)	1919	—	17955
80A	4–4–0	Clyde Loco. Co.	(5)	1886	Stafford	—
81	4–6–0	Hawthorn Leslie	(3373)	1919	—	17956
81A	4–4–0	Clyde Loco. Co.	(6)	1886	Colville	—
82	4–6–0	Hawthorn Leslie	(3374)	1919	—	17957
82A	4–4–0	Clyde Loco. Co.	(7)	1886	—	14278
83A	4–4–0	"	(8)	1886	Monkland	—
84A	4–4–0	Lochgorm	—	1888	Dochfour	—
85A	4–4–0	"	—	1892	—	—
86	4–4–0	"	—	1893	—	14279
87	4–4–0	"	—	1893	—	(14280)
88	4–4–0	"	—	1895	—	(14281)
89	4–4–0	Neilson	(4428)	1892	Sir George	14271
90A	4–4–0	"	(4429)	1892	Grandtully	—
91A	4–4–0	"	(4430)	1892	Strathspey	—
92A	4–4–0	"	(4431)	1892	Strathdearn	14272
93A	4–4–0	"	(4432)	1892	Strathnairn	—

No.	Type	Builder	Works No.	Building Date	Name	LMS No.
94	4–4–0	Neilson	(4433)	1892	Strathtay	(14273)
95	4–4–0	"	(4434)	1892	Strathcarron	14274
96A	4–4–0	"	(4435)	1892	Glentilt	—
97A	4–4–0	"	(4436)	1892	Glenmore	—
98	4–4–0	"	(4437)	1892	Glentruim	14275
99A	4–4–0	"	(4438)	1892	Glentromie	—
100	4–4–0	"	(4439)	1892	Glenbruar	14276
101	4–4–0T	Dubs	(2778)	1892	—	15013
102	4–4–0T	"	(2779)	1892	Munlochy	15014
103	4–6–0	Sharp Stewart	(4022)	1894	—	17916
104	4–6–0	"	(4023)	1894	—	17917
105	4–6–0	"	(4024)	1894	—	17918
106	4–6–0	"	(4025)	1894	—	17919
107	4–6–0	"	(4026)	1894	—	17920
108	4–6–0	"	(4027)	1894	—	17921
109	4–6–0	"	(4028)	1894	—	17922
110	4–6–0	"	(4029)	1894	—	17923
111	4–6–0	"	(4030)	1894	—	17924
112	4–6–0	"	(4031)	1894	—	17925
113	4–6–0	"	(4032)	1894	—	17926
114	4–6–0	"	(4033)	1894	—	17927
115	4–6–0	"	(4034)	1894	—	17928
116	4–6–0	"	(4035)	1894	—	17929
117	4–6–0	"	(4036)	1894	—	17930
118A	2–4–0T	Kitson	(1706)	1870	—	—
119	4–4–0	Dubs	(3392)	1896	Loch Insh	14379
120	4–4–0	"	(3393)	1896	Loch Ness	14380
121	4–4–0	"	(3394)	1896	Loch Ericht	14381
122	4–4–0	"	(3395)	1896	Loch Moy	14382
123	4–4–0	"	(3396)	1896	Loch An Dorb	14383
124	4–4–0	"	(3397)	1896	Loch Laggan	14384
125	4–4–0	"	(3398)	1896	Loch Tay	14385
126	4–4–0	"	(3399)	1896	Loch Tummel	14386
127	4–4–0	"	(3400)	1896	Loch Garry	14387
128	4–4–0	"	(3401)	1896	Loch Luichart	14388
129	4–4–0	"	(3402)	1896	Loch Maree	14389
130	4–4–0	"	(3403)	1896	Loch Fannich	14390
131	4–4–0	"	(3404)	1896	Loch Shin	14391
132	4–4–0	"	(3405)	1896	Loch Navar	14392
133	4–4–0	"	(3406)	1896	Loch Laoghal	14393
134	0–6–0	"	(3842)	1900	—	17693
135	0–6–0	"	(3843)	1900	—	17694
136	0–6–0	"	(3844)	1900	—	17695
137	0–6–0	"	(3845)	1900	—	17696
138	0–6–0	"	(3846)	1900	—	17697
139	0–6–0	"	(3847)	1900	—	17698
140	4–6–0	"	(3848)	1900	Taymouth Castle	14675
141	4–6–0	"	(3849)	1900	Ballindalloch Castle	14676
142	4–6–0	"	(3850)	1900	Dunrobin Castle	14677
143	4–6–0	"	(3851)	1900	Gordon Castle	14678
144	4–6–0	"	(3852)	1900	Blair Castle	14679
145	4–6–0	"	(3853)	1900	Murthly Castle	14680
146	4–6–0	"	(4244)	1902	Skibo Castle	14681
147	4–6–0	"	(4245)	1902	Beaufort Castle	14682
148	4–6–0	"	(4246)	1902	Cawdor Castle	14683
149	4–6–0	"	(4247)	1902	Duncraig Castle	14684

APPENDIX 3

LOCOMOTIVES OF THE FORMER HIGHLAND RAILWAY, 31 DECEMBER 1947

No.	*Type*	*Builder*	*Works No.*	*Building Date*	*Name*	*LMS No.*
1	4–4–0	Dübs	(3685)	1898	Ben-y-Gloe	14397
2	4–4–0	"	(3686)	1898	Ben Alder	14398
3	4–4–0	"	(3687)	1898	Ben Wyvis	14399
5	4–4–0	"	(3689)	1899	Ben Vrackie	14401
7	4–4–0	"	(3691)	1899	Ben Attow	14403
8	4–4–0	"	(3692)	1899	Ben Clebrig	14404
13	4–4–0	Lochgorm	—	1900	Ben Alisky	14409
14	4–4–0	"	—	1900	Ben Dearg	14410
18	0–6–0	Dübs	(4240)	1902	—	17699
21	0–6–0	"	(4243)	1902	—	17702
25	0–4–4T	Lochgorm	—	1905	—	14051
41	4–4–0	N.B. Loco Co.	(17399)	1906	Ben Bach Ard	14415
45	0–4–4T	Lochgorm	—	1905	—	15053
47	4–4–0	N.B. Loco. Co.	(17400)	1906	Ben a'Bhuird	14416
52	4–6–0	Hawthorn Leslie	(3331)	1919	Clan Munro	14764
55	4–6–0	"	(3444)	1921	Clan Mackinnon	14767
75	4–6–0	"	(3286)	1918	—	17950
76	4–6–0	"	(3287)	1918	—	17951
78	4–6–0	"	(3289)	1918	—	17953
79	4–6–0	"	(3371)	1919	—	17954
80	4–6–0	"	(3372)	1919	—	17955
81	4–6–0	"	(3373)	1919	—	17956
119	4–4–0	Dübs	(3392)	1896	Loch Insh	14379
125	4–4–0	"	(3398)	1896	Loch Tay	14385
134	0–6–0	"	(3842)	1900	—	17693
135	0–6–0	"	(3843)	1900	—	17694
136	0–6–0	"	(3844)	1900		17695
138	0–6–0	"	(3846)	1900	—	17697
139	0–6–0	"	(3847)	1900	—	17698

APPENDIX 4

CYLINDERS AND GEARS

Class	*Cylinders dia x stroke*		*Throw of eccentric*	*Ports Length*	*Ports Breadth steam*	*Ports Breadth exhaust*	*Gears*	*Remarks*
	in	*in*	*in*	*in*	*in*	*in*		
Raigmore (I)	15	20					Allan	No. 1 Rebt. with 15½ x 21 cyl.
Seafield	16	22						Rebt. with 16 x 24 cyl and Nos 7 & 10 to 17 x 24
Belladrum	16	20					Allan	
No. 14	16	22					Allan	Rebt. with 17 x 24 cyl at 6 - 1 crs
No. 16	12	18					Neilson indirect	Rebt. with Stephenson gear in 1866
No. 17	13	18						
No. 18	17	22	5½	12½	1¼	2¾	Allan	Rebt. with 18 x 24 cyl.
Glenbarry	17	22		12½	1¼	2¾	Allan	(2) Rebt. with 18 x 24 cyl.
No. 36	17	24	5¾	12½	1¼	2¾	Allan	Rebt. with 18 x 24 cyl.
Lochgorm tank	14	20					Stephenson	
No. 2	15½	22					Allan	
Duke/Lochgorm/Clyde	18	24	6	15	1½	3	Allan	
Raigmore (II)	16	22					Allan	
Jones tank	16	24		13	1¼	2	Allan	
Skye bogie	18	24			1½		Allan	
No. 13	14	20						
Strath	18	24	6	15	1½	3	Allan	
Yankee tank	16	22					Stephenson	
Big Goods	20	26	6½	16	1 5/8	3¼	Allan	(3)
Special tank	10	18					Stephenson	
Special tank rebuilt	12	18						
Dunrobin (II)	13	18	5½	10	1 1/8	2¼	Allan	
Loch	19	24		piston			Allan	
Small and Big Bens	18¼	26	6½	2 x 8	1 5/8	3¼	Stephenson	(4) Steam reverser
Barney	18¼	26	6½	2 x 8	1 5/8	3¼	Stephenson	
Castle I and II	19½	26	7	16	1 5/8	3¼	Allan	Steam reverser
Castle III	19½	26	7	16	1 5/8	3¼	Allan	Screw reverser
Scrap tank	18	24					Stephenson	
Passenger tank	14	20		10	1¼	2	Stephenson	
Banking tank	18¼	26	6½	2 x 8	1 5/8	3¼	Stephenson	Steam reverser
River	21	28		10 inch piston			Walschaert	Steam reverser
No. 73	20	26		10 inch piston			Walschaert	Screw reverser
Superheated Goods	20½	26		10 inch piston			Walschaert	Nos 75-78 lever and Nos 79-82 screw reverser
Clan	21	26		10 inch piston			Walschaert	Screw reverser

NOTES
1. Lever operated reversers were fitted unless otherwise noted.
2. When built Nos 30 to 35 inclusive were provided with 16½ by 22 inch cylinders.
3. Later lined up to 19 by 26 inches by P. Drummond.
4. Nos 1 to 8 inclusive initially equipped with lever reverse, the reach rod, passing beneath the driving wheel axles to a rocker pivoted on an extension from the frames on the LHS between the bogie and leading driving wheel. These were all altered to steam reverser before World War I.

APPENDIX 5

BASIC DIMENSIONS

Class	*Wheel arrangement*	*Length over buffers* ft in	*Total wheel base (engine & tender)* ft in	*Height above chimney* ft in	*Rail boiler C.L.* ft in	*Width over* *platform* ft in	*cab sides* ft in	*Weight in WO* *adhesive* T C	*Total (inc. tender)* T C	*Tractive effort (at 85% WP)* lb	*(1)*
Raigmore (I)	2–2–2								c43 - 0	5.312	
No. 1 rebt.	2–4–0									5,956	
Seafield	2–4–0				5 - 10½			18 - 10	44 - 0	9,574/10,445	
No. 7 & 10 rebt.	4–4–0				5 - 10½			20 - 10	56 - 10	11,791	
Belladrum	2–2–2								45 - 0	7,253	
No. 12 rebt.	2–2–2T		14 - 2					12 - 0	29 - 0	7,253	
No. 14	2–4–0				5 - 10½			21 - 0	46 - 10	9,574/11,320	
No. 16	0–4–0T		5 - 9					16 - 0	16 - 0	6,295	
No. 17	0–4–0T		6 - 0					16 - 8	16 - 8	5,387	
No. 17 rebt.	0–4–2T	22 - 8	12 - 0					14 - 0	20 - 0	5,387	
No. 18	2–4–0		35 - 3	13 - 0	6 - 4½	6 - 10 5/8	6 - 2	22 - 0	56 - 0	13,181	
No. 18 rebt.	2–4–0	47 - 4½	35 - 3	13 - 0	6 - 6	6 - 10 5/8		25 - 0	59 - 10	15,737	
Glenbarry	2–2–2			13 - 0	5 - 11¾	6 - 10¾	6 - 2	14 - 0	55 - 0	8,823	
Glenbarry rebt.	2–4–0	48 - 2	35 - 9	13 - 0	6 - 5½			26 - 10	67 - 10	13, 219	(2)
No. 36	2–4–0	47 - 7½	35 - 6	13 - 0	6 - 4½	6 - 10 5/8	6 - 2	23 - 0	57 - 0	14,380	
No. 36 rebt.	2–4–0				6 - 6	6 - 10 5/8		25 - 10	60 - 10	16,786	
Lochgorm tank	0–6–0T	25 - 3	12 - 0	11 - 6	5 - 4½			23 - 10	23 - 10	9,299/9,087	
No. 56 rebt.	0–6–0T	25 - 3	12 - 0	11 - 6	5 - 5			26 - 0	26 - 0	9,845	
No. 2	2–4–0		34 - 3		5 - 6½			19 - 10		7,787	
Duke	4–4–0	51 - 3	41 - 6	13 - 0 5/8	6 - 7	7 - 1	6 - 5	26 - 10	72 - 0	12,338	(3)
Lochgorm bogie	4–4–0	53 - 9	44 - 0	13 - 0	6 - 6	7 - 1	6 - 5	26 - 10	72 - 0	13,220	
Raigmore (II)	2–4–0	47 - 3	34 - 3		6 - 3½			23 - 0	62 - 0	9,749	
Jones tank	2–4–0T	30 - 4	14 - 1	11 - 10½	5 - 9	7 - 6	6 - 10½	25 - 0	36 - 0	12,827	
Jones tank rebt.	4–4–0T			11 - 10½	5 - 9	7 - 6	6 - 10½		37 - 12	12,827	(4)
Skye bogie	4–4–0	52 - 7	42 - 9	c12 - 8	6 - 3	7 - 1	6 - 5	28 - 0	73 - 0	16,121/15,613	
Clyde bogie	4–4–0	54 - 1½	44 - 0	13 - 0	6 - 7¼	7 - 1		28 - 0	74 - 10	14,007	
No. 13	0–4–4ST	29 - 6	18 - 0		5 - 9			20 - 0	32 - 0	6,533	
No. 53 rebt.	0–4–4T	29 - 6	18 - 0	11 - 4	6 - 0			19 - 10	34 - 0	9,147	
Strath	4–4–0	54 - 1 7/16	43 - 11 15/16	13 - 1 1/8	7 - 4	7 - 1	6 - 5	29 - 3	76 - 2	14,007	(5)
No. 101	4–4–0T	31 - 1	20 - 3	13 - 0	6 - 8	8 - 8			41 - 12	10,638	
No. 102 rebt.	4–4–0T	31 - 1	20 - 3					30 - 5	44 - 0	12,158	
Yankee tank	4–4–0T	31 - 1	20 - 3	13 - 0	6 - 8	8 - 8		29 - 0	42 - 10	10,638	
Big Goods	4–6–0	58 - 5½	48 - 5½	13 - 0	7 - 4	8 - 4	7 - 0	42 - 0	94 - 7	23,666/24,362	
Special tank	2–4–0T	25 - 0	11 - 9		5 - 4			16 - 0	21 - 0	4,462	
Special tank rebt.	2–4–0T	25 - 0	11 - 9	11 - 3	5 - 8			17 - 0	24 - 0	6,426	
Dunrobin (II)	0–4–4T		18 - 1½	11 - 9	6 - 0	7 - 6	7 - 0	16 - 2	25 - 5	7,183	
Loch	4–4–0	54 - 7½	44 - 9	13 - 0½	7 - 5	8 - 0	7 - 0	31 - 10	87 - 7	17,070	(6)
Loch rebt.	4–4–0	54 - 7½	44 - 9	12 - 9	8 - 2	8 - 0	7 - 0	32 - 0	88 - 6	17,070/17,558	
Small Ben	4–4–0	53 - 6	44 - 1½	13 - 0	7 - 6	7 - 4½	6 - 1¾	31 - 4	83 - 10	17,890	(7)
Small Ben rebt.	4–4–0	53 - 6	44 - 1½	12 - 10½	7 - 6	7 - 4½	6 - 1¾	31 - 14	84 - 7	7,070/18,401	(7)
Barney	0–6–0	53 - 4	41 - 8½	13 - 0	7 - 3	7 - 4½	6 - 1¾	43 - 0	83 - 0	21,469	(8)
Castle I	4–6–0	60 - 7	52 - 5½	13 - 2	8 - 2	8 - 4½	6 - 9	44 - 17	103 - 6	21,922	(5)
Castle II	4–6–0	61 - 2	52 - 5½	13 - 3¾	8 - 2	8 - 4½	6 - 9	44 - 18	104 - 8	21,922	(5)
Castle III	4–6–0	60 - 9½	50 - 10	13 - 3¾	8 - 3½	8 - 4½	6 - 9	45 - 17	107 - 0	21,008/20,425	(5)
Scrap tank	0–6–0T	30 - 8½	14 - 2	13 - 0	6 - 11			47 - 18	47 - 18	16,921	
Passenger tank	0–4–4T	28 - 7¼	18 - 3	11 - 4	6 - 3	7 - 7		21 - 10	35 - 15	9,256	
Big Ben	4–4–0	56 - 3	47 - 5½	13 - 0	8 - 2	7 - 4½	6 - 9	32 - 3	94 - 13	18,401/17,890	(9)
Banking tank	0–6–4T	38 - 8½	27 - 3	12 - 9	8 - 0	8 - 2	7 - 8	49 - 10	69 - 0	22,082/21,469	
River	4–6–0	59 - 6	49 - 4½	13 - 3¾	8 - 8½	8 - 9½	8 - 1	52 - 10	119 - 6	23,324	(10)
No. 73	4–4–0	55 - 7	46 - 5½	12 - 10	8 - 8	8 - 8	8 - 0	34 - 5	98 - 3	18,859/20,627	
Superheated Goods	4–6–0	55 - 5	46 - 6	12 - 10	8 - 8	8 - 11	8 - 0	41 - 14	92 - 2	23,587/25,799	
Clan	4–6–0	59 - 3	50 - 0	12 - 10	8 - 9	8 - 11	8 - 0	45 - 8	104 - 6	23,012/23,688	

NOTES TO APPENDIX 5 (Basic Dimensions)

1. A double entry under the heading of tractive effort indicates that the wheel diameter or boiler pressure has been altered during the life of the locomotives.
2. The second entry for the 'Glenbarry' class shows the dimensions after conversion to 2–4–0s, the fitting of enlarged cylinders and Jones boilers. However it should be noted that these modifications were not necessarily all put in hand at one time and the adhesive and total weights of a converted locomotive with an original boiler were respectively 25 tons and 61 ton 10 cwt.
3. Adhesive weight 27 tons after fitting vacuum brake.
4. Total weight of No. 17 was 39 ton 10 cwt after rebuilding with 850 gallon water tanks.
5. Height to chimney top cut down to 13 feet after grouping.
6. The adhesive and total weights of the 'Lochs' built with 3,100 gallon tenders in 1917 were respectively 32 ton 14 cwt and 87 ton 14 cwt.
7. When coupled to 3,000 gallon six wheeled tenders.
8. When coupled to 3,200 gallon bogie tenders. On being fitted with Caledonian Rly boilers the height to the top of the chimney was reduced to 12 ft 10½ in and the adhesive and total weights each increased by 10 cwt.
9. When coupled to 3,600 gallon bogie tenders. The adhesive and total weights increased respectively to 35 ton 13 cwt and 95 ton 9 cwt when fitted with superheated boilers from 1923 on.
10. Height to top of chimney cut down to 12 ft 10 in on being purchased by the Caledonian Rly in 1915, although the maximum height then became 12 ft 10 7/8 in over the dome.

APPENDIX 6

BOILER DIMENSIONS

Class	Max ext dia. ft in	Length between tubeplates ft in	Length outer FB casing ft in	Depth of FB below BCL front ft in	Depth of FB below BCL rear ft in	Working pressure lb/sq in	Tubes No.	Tubes dia. in	Heating surface tubes sq ft	Heating surface firebox sq ft	Cross tubes /super heater sq ft	Tubes/ flues No.	Tubes/ flues dia.	Grate area sq ft	
Raigmore (I)	3 - 7		4 - 2¼			100	162	1¼			—	—		12.25	
Seafield	4 - 1	11 - 2	4 - 2½			120	218	1¾	1115	74	—	—		12.25	
Belladrum	3 - 6½					120	158	1¾			—	—		15.5	
No. 14	4 - 1		5 - 10½			120					—	—		15.5	(1)
No. 16						120			353	39	—	—		12.0	
No. 17						100			425	53	—	—			
No. 18	4 - 1	9 - 9	5 - 10 3/8	3 - 9¼	3 - 9¼	150	235	1¾	1049	114	—	—		16.0	(1)
No. 18 rebt.	4 - 1		5 - 6	4 - 3	4 - 3	140	223	1¾	985	93	—	—		16.2	
Glenbarry	3 - 11	10 - 0½	6 - 1 3/8	3 - 6½	3 - 6½	120	204	1¾	964	115	—	—		20.33	(2)
Glenbarry rebt.	4 - 0	10 - 8 3/8	5 - 5½	4 - 6	4 - 6	150	223	1¾	1093	93	—	—		16.2	
No. 36	4 - 1	10 - 6	5 - 2 7/8	3 - 10½	3 - 10½	150	{ 252 2	1¾ 1½	1220	81	294	—		15.5	
No. 36 rebt.						160	223	1¾	1045	93	—	—		16.2	
Lochgorm tank	3 - 7+	8 - 2½	4 - 2¼			120	162	1¾	608	63	—	—		12.25	
Lochgorm tank rebt.						120	158	1¾	578	64	—	—		12.5	(3)
No. 2 rebt.	3 - 7	10 - 1¾	4 - 6			130	181	1¾	836	70	—	—		13.5	
Duke	4 - 2	11 - 0 7/8	5 - 5½	4 - 6	4 - 6	140	223	1¾	1132	96	—	—		16.25	(4)
Lochgorm bogie	4 - 2	11 - 0	5 - 5½	4 - 6	4 - 6	150	210	1¾	1058	93	—	—		16.25	
Raigmore (II)	4 - 1					140	223	1¾	1004	93	—	—		16.2	
Jones tank	3 - 7 7/8	9 - 11	4 - 6	3 - 8	3 - 8	140	181	1¾	820	93	—	—		16.2	
Skye bogie	4 - 2	11 - 0	5 - 5½	4 - 2¾	4 - 2¾	150	212	1¾	1123	93	—	—		16.2	
Clyde bogie	4 - 2	10 - 4	6 - 2½	4 - 6	4 - 6	160	223	1¾	1038	102	—	—		18.83	(5)
No. 13	3 - 6½					100	158	1¾	578	62	—	—		12.5	
No. 53 rebt.						140			623	67	—	—		13.0	
Strath	4 - 6	10 - 2	6 - 2½	5 - 1 3/8	5 - 1 3/8	160	242	1¾	1127	115	—	—		18.83	
Yankee tank	3 - 11¾	10 - 9 5/8	4 - 10	4 - 5	4 - 5	160	150	1 7/8	795	88	—	—		14.0	(6)
Big Goods	4 - 9	14 - 1 3/8	7 - 9	4 - 10¼	3 - 7¾	175	211	2	1559	113	—	—		22.6	(7)
Special tank	2 - 6¾		2 - 10			140	75	1¾	341	38	—	—		6.25	
Special tank rebt.			3 - 1	4 - 0	4 - 0	140	113	1¾	503	49	—	—		8.4	
Dunrobin (II)	3 - 4¼	8 - 4 1/8	3 - 11	4 - 3	4 - 0	150	130	1¾	517	58	—	—		11	
Loch	4 - 7	10 - 6 1/8	6 - 8½	5 - 2¼	4 - 10¾	175	244	1¾	1175	116	—	—		20.5	
Loch rebt.	4 - 9¼	10 - 7	6 - 5	5 - 5¾	5 - 0	175	275	1¾	1333	119	—	—		20.0	(9)
Small Ben	4 - 6¼	10 - 9 7/8	6 - 4	5 - 2¾	4 - 8¾	175	214	1¾	1061	117	—	—		20.37	(10)
Small Ben rebt.	4 - 6¼	10 - 7	6 - 2 3/8	5 - 2¾	4 - 8¾	175	222	1¾	1076	112	—	—		19.5	(9)
Barney	4 - 6¼	10 - 9 7/8	6 - 4	5 - 2¾	4 - 8¾	175	214	1¾	1061	115	129	35	2¾	20.37	
Barney rebt.	4 - 6¼	10 - 7	6 - 2 3/8	5 - 2¾	4 - 8¾	175	222	1¾	1076	112	—	—		19.5	
Castle I	5 - 0	14 - 9 1/8	8 - 0	5 - 3¾	3 - 11¾	180	248	2	1916	134	—	—		26.0	(8)
Castle II & III	5 - 0	14 - 9 1/8	8 - 0	5 - 4	4 - 0	180	248	2	1916	132	—	—		25.5	(8)
Castle LMS	5 - 0	14 - 9 1/8	8 - 0	5 - 4	4 - 0	180	292	1¾	1974	134	—	—		26.5	(11)
Scrap tank	4 - 0	10 - 8 3/8	5 - 5½	4 - 4	4 - 4	160	223	1¾	1093	93	—	—		16.2	
Passenger tank	4 - 0	8 - 5¼	4 - 2½	3 - 10½	3 - 10½	150	170	1¾	652	67.5	—	—		13.0	
Big Ben	5 - 3	10 - 10¾	6 - 4	5 - 10¾	5 - 4¾	180	266	2	1516	132	—	—		20.3	(8)
Big Ben Suph.	5 - 3	10 - 10¾	6 - 4	5 - 10¾	5 - 4¾	175			1018	132	168	19		20.3	
Banking tank	4 - 6¼	10 - 10¾	7 - 0	5 - 2¾	4 - 5	180	230	1¾	1148	120	—	—		22.43	(8)
Banking tank rebt.	4 - 6¼	11 - 0	7 - 0			180	227	1¾	1144	110	—	—		22.5	(8)
River	5 - 3	14 - 9 1/8	8 - 0	5 - 6	4 - 4	160	129	2	1460	140	350	24	5	25.3	(12)
No. 73	4 - 9 11/16	11 - 4 5/8	7 - 0½			160	118	2	1016	124	180	21	5	22.5	(8)
Superheated Goods	4 - 7 11/16	14 - 1 5/8	7 - 1	5 - 8	4 - 6	160	92	2	1069	127	241	21	5	22.75	(8)
Clan	4 - 9 13/16	14 - 10 5/8	8 - 0	5 - 6	4 - 2½	170	118	2	1328	139	256	21	5	25.5	(8)

NOTES TO APPENDIX 6 (Boiler Dimensions)

1. Firebox of Beattie type divided into two parts by transverse mid-feather.
2. Nos 28 to 35 inclusive had a longitudinal mid-feather in the firebox and two firedoors. Nos 46 to 54 inclusive on the other hand had the transverse mid-feather similar to the 2–4–0s, while No. 55 had a conventional firebox.
3. Boiler pressure on No. 56 raised to 130 lb/sq.in. in 1902.
4. Boiler pressure later raised to 150 lb/sq.in.
5. Boiler pressure on No. 81 increased to 170 lb/sq.in. in 1916.
6. Nos 101 and 102 originally had boilers pressed to 140 lb sq.in. No. 102 was fitted with a new larger boiler in 1906 of which no details are known other than that the pressure was 160 lb/sq.in.
7. The arrangement of tubes was altered first to 207 and later 203 in number.
8. Boiler pressure later altered to 175 lb/sq.in.
9. Boiler pressure sometimes quoted as 180 lb/sq.in.
10. Number of tubes later reduced to 210.
11. Direct stay fireboxes.
12. Originally equipped with feed water pre-heaters and drop grates.

APPENDIX 7

FRAMES AND MOTION

Class	Frames Length ft in	Frames Thickness in	Bogie ft in	Wheel base Coupled ft in	Wheel base Total ft in	Cylinder centre to centre	Lengths centre to centre: connecting rods ft in	Lengths centre to centre: eccentrics ft in	Wheel diameter & No. of spokes: leading/trailing or bogie ft in	No.	driving ft in	No.	Driving journals diameter in	Driving journals length in	
Raigmore (I)			—	—					3 - 6	10	6 - 0	19			
No. 1 rebuilt			—	6 - 11	13 - 9				3 - 6	10	6 - 0	19			
Seafield			—	8 - 4	14 - 3				3 - 6	10	5 - 0	15			
Rebt. Nos 7 & 10			5 - 6	8 - 4	20 - 6				2 - 6	8	5 - 0	15			
Belladrum			—	—	14 - 2				3 - 6	10	6 - 0	19			
No. 14	23 - 5		—	8 - 4	14 - 3				3 - 0	10	5 - 0	15			(1)
No. 16			—	5 - 9	5 - 9				—	—	3 - 6	8			
No. 17	18 - 9		—	6 - 0	12 - 0 (2)				3 - 1 (2)	10	4 - 0	12			
No. 18	23 - 11	1	—	9 - 0	15 - 0	6 - 2	5 - 6	3 - 8¼	3 - 7½	10	5 - 1½	15	7	7	(3)
Glenbarry	22 - 3½	1	—	—	14 - 6	6 - 2	6 - 2	4-1¼ / 4-2	3 - 7½	10	6 - 1½	19	7	7	
Glenbarry rebt.			—	8 - 9	15 - 6				3 - 9	10	6 - 3	19			
No. 36	24 - 2	1	—	9 - 3	15 - 6	6 - 2	5 - 8	3 - 11¼	3 - 7½	10	5 - 1½	15	7	7	(3)
Lochgorm tank			—	6-0+6-0	12 - 0	2 - 3			—	—	3 - 7	8			(4)
No. 2			—						3 - 9	10	6 - 3	19			
Duke/Lochgorm	27 - 9	1¼	6 - 0	8 - 9	21 - 6	6 - 3	6 - 4¾	4 - 3¾	3 - 9½	10	6 - 3½	19	7	7	(5)
Raigmore (II)				8 - 4	14 - 6	6 - 3			3 - 9	10	6 - 3	19			
Clyde Bogie	27 - 10½	1¼	6 - 0	8 - 9	21 - 6	6 - 3	6 - 5	4 - 3¾	3 - 9½	10	6 - 3½	19	8	7½	
Jones tank	25 - 8½	1	—	8 - 4	14 - 1	6 - 1	5 - 6½	3 - 10¾	3 - 9½	10	4 - 9½	13	6¼	6½	
Jones tank rebt.		1	5 - 6	8 - 4		6 - 1	5 - 6½	3 - 10¾	2 - 7½	8	4 - 9	13	6¼	6½	
Skye bogie	27 - 6	1¼	6 - 0	8 - 9	21 - 6	6 - 3	6 - 5	4 - 3¾	3 - 3½	8	5 - 3½	15	7	7	
No. 13	25 - 0		5 - 6	6 - 0	18 - 0	2 - 3			2 - 7½	8	4 - 3	12			
Strath	27 - 10½	1¼	6 - 0	8 - 9	21 - 6	6 - 3	6 - 5	4 - 3¾	3 - 9½	10	6 - 3½	19	8	7½	
Yankee tank	27 - 5	1	5 - 9	7 - 2	20 - 3	6 - 2	6 - 4	4-1½ / 4-1 3/16	3 - 0	10	5 - 3	15	8	7	(6)
Big Goods	32 - 11	1¼	6 - 6	5-6+7-9	25 - 0	6 - 7	9 - 4	8 - 1½	3 - 2½	8	5 - 3½	15	7½	7½	(7) (8)
Special tank	22 - 1		—	5 - 9	11 - 9	6 - 1½			3 - 0	10	4 - 0	12			(9)
Dunrobin (II)	24 - 6	7/8	5 - 0	6 - 3	18 - 1½	2 - 4	5 - 1	3-6 / 3-6 7/32	2 - 6	8	4 - 6	14	5¾	7	
Loch	29 - 2	1¼	6 - 6	9 - 0	22 - 6	6 - 4½	6 - 8	4-7 7/16 / 4-7½	3 - 3	8	6 - 3½	19	8	8½	(6)
Small & Big Bens	28 - 4	1	6 - 6	9 - 0	22 - 3	2 - 3	6 - 6	5 - 6	3 - 6	10	6 - 0	19	8	7½	(10)
Barney	26 - 0	1	—	7-6+9-0	16 - 6	2 - 3	6 - 6	5 - 6	—	—	5 - 0	15	8	7½	
Castle I & II	33 - 3	1 1/8	6 - 6	6-0+8-3	26 - 3	6 - 7	10 - 3	8-1½ / 8-1	3 - 3	8	5 - 9	17	8	7½	(6) (7) (11)
Castle III	33 - 7½	1 1/8	6 - 6	6-3+8-3	26 - 7½	6 - 7	10 - 7½	8-6 / 8-6 1/16	3 - 3	8	6 - 0	18	8	8½	(6) (7)
Scrap tank			—	6-4+7-10	14 - 2				—	—	5 - 2½	15			
Passenger tank	25 - 6	7/8	5 - 0	6 - 0	18 - 3	2 - 3	4 - 10	4 - 0	2 - 6	8	4 - 6	13	6	7	
Banking tank	35 - 0	1	6 - 6	7-6+8-0	27 - 3		6 - 6		3 - 3	8	5 - 0	15	8	7½	(10)
River	33 - 7½	1 1/8	6 - 6	6-3+8-0	26 - 4½	6 - 8½	10 - 3½	4 - 7 5/8	3 - 3	10	6 - 0	20	8	8½	(12)
No. 73	29 - 8½		6 - 7	8 - 9	22 - 11½				3 - 3	10	6 - 3	20	8	8½	
Superheated Goods	31 - 10	1 1/16	6 - 7	6-0+6-6	24 - 1	6 - 8½	9 - 10		3 - 0	9	5 - 3	16	8	7¼	
Clan	33 - 6	1 1/8	6 - 7	6-9+7-3	25 - 9	6 - 9	10 - 8	5 - 6¼	3 - 0	9	6 - 0	19	8	8½	

NOTES TO APPENDIX 7 (Frames and motion)

1. Wheel diameters later increased to 3 ft 2½ in. and 5 ft 2½ in.
2. On being rebuilt as a 0—4—2T in 1867.
3. Wheel diameter later increased to 3 ft 9 in. and 5 ft 3 in.
4. No. 56 had webs between the spokes of all wheels, while Nos 57 and 16 only had webs to the centre wheels. Wheel diameter altered to 3 ft 8 in. on fitting new tyres.
5. The length of the connecting rods of the Lochgorm class were 6 ft 5 in. and the bogie wheels 3 ft 8½ in. dia.
6. Length of forward eccentric quoted followed by backward.
7. Middle driving wheels originally flangeless, flanged tyres fitted later.
8. Diameter of journal to driving axle 8 inches.
9. Before rebuilding in 1896.
10. Frames cranked over bogie.
11. The length of the driving journal of the 'Castle' II was 8½ inches.
12. Driving axle journal 8½ inches dia. by 10 inches long.

APPENDIX 8

TENDERS

Attached to:	Year	Capacities Water gall	Capacities Coal T	Wheel base ft in	Outside frames Length ft in	Outside frames Depth ft in	Tank Length ft in	Tank Breadth ft in	Tank Depth ft in	Well Length ft in	Well Width ft in	Well Depth ft in	Platform Width ft in	Wheels No.	Wheels Dia. ft in	Weight in WO T C	
Raigmore (I), No. 12	1855	1,100	2½	8 - 0						—				4	3 - 6	16 - 0	
Seafield, No. 14	1858	1,200	2½	8 - 3						—				4	3 - 6	16 0	
No. 18, Glenbarry No. 36, Raigmore II	1863	1,800	3	11 - 3						—				6	3 - 7½	24 - 0	(1)
Duke	1874	1,800	4	11 - 0	18 - 6			7 - 4		—			7 - 4	6	3 - 9	30 - 0	
Skye Bogie	1882	2,100	4	12 - 0						—				6	3 9	30 - 0	
Lochgorm/Clyde	1883	2,250	4	13 - 0	21 - 0	2 - 7½	16 - 6	7 - 3	3 - 4½	—			7 - 3	6	3 - 9½	31 - 10	
Strath	1892	2,250	4½	13 - 0	21 - 0	2 - 7½	16 - 6½	7 - 3	3 - 4¾	—			7 - 3	6	3 9½	31 - 0	
Big Goods Loch	1894	3,000	5	13 - 0	21 - 0	2 - 9¼	18 - 6	7 - 9	3 - 10½	—			8 - 4	6	3 - 9½	38 - 7	
Loch	1917	3, 100	5	13 - 0	21 - 0	2 - 9¼	19 - 5	7 - 9	3 - 10½	—			8 - 0	6	3 - 9½	37 - 2	
Small Ben	1898	3,000	5	13 - 0	21 - 4	2 - 5	18 - 1	7 - 2¼	3 - 9	14 - 0	3 - 11	1 - 4½	7 - 4½	6	4 0	37 - 10	
Barney	1906	3,185	5	13 - 0	21 - 4	2 - 5	19 - 2¼	7 - 2¼	3 - 9	14 - 0	3 - 11	1 - 4½	7 - 4½	6	4 - 0	38 7	
Barney	1900	3,200	6	16 - 6	23 - 6	1 - 1½	21 - 6½	7 - 2¾	3 - 10	9 - 0	3 - 9	0 - 10½	7 - 4½	8	3 - 6	43 0	
Big Ben	1909	3,600	6	16 - 6			21 - 6½	7 - 2¾		9 - 0	3 - 9			8	3 - 6	45 - 5	
Castle I & II	1900	3,350	5	16 - 6	23 - 6	1 - 6	21 - 6½	7 - 7¾	3 - 11½	—			8 - 4½	8	3 - 6	44 - 9	(2)
Castle III	1917	4,000	6½	13 - 6	22 - 9	2 - 5	20 - 9	7 - 8½						6	4 - 0	46 - 7	(3)
River	1915	4,000	6½	13 - 0	21 - 4	2 - 5	19 - 2¾	7 - 8¼	5 - 6	14 - 0	3 - 11	1 - 4½	7 - 10¼	6	4 - 0	47 - 10	
No. 73	1917	3,500	7	13 - 0	21 - 4	2 - 9½	19 - 1½	7 - 11½	4 - 6	—			8 - 8	6	4 - 0	43 - 3	
Superheated Goods	1917	3,000	5	12 - 0	19 - 2	3 - 0	17 - 1½	7 - 11½	4 - 2	—			8 - 8	6	3 - 9	35 - 13	
Clan	1919	3,500	7	13 - 0	21 - 4	2 - 9½	19 - 1½	7 - 11½	4 - 6	—			8 - 8	6	4 - 0	42 - 2	

NOTES

1. Wheel diameter later altered to 3 ft 9 in.
2. Coal capacity originally 6 tons on Castle IIs.
3. Dimension of tender well not known.

APPENDIX 9

TANK ENGINE WATER & COAL CAPACITIES

Type	Water gall	Coal T
No. 12 rebt.		
No. 16	530	
No. 17	510	¾
Lochgorm tank	750	¾/1¼
No. 56 rebt.		
Jones tank	700	1¼
No. 17 rebt.	850	1¼
No. 13	820	1½
No. 53 rebt.	900	1½
No. 101	700	1½
No. 102 rebt.	900	1½
Yankee tank	900	1½
Special tank	400	½
Special tank rebt.	560	¾
Dunrobin (II)	700	
Scrap tank	1,000	1¾
Passenger tank	900	1¼
Banking tank	1,970	4½

APPENDIX 10

PROJECTED DESIGNS BY P DRUMMOND

Type	4–4–0	4–4–0	0–4–4T	0–4–4T	0–8–0	0–8–0
Date of drawing	22/12/99	8/4/01	28/3/02	u/k	3/11/02	5/12/02
Cylinders dia x stroke (in)	18½ x 26	19 x 26	17 x 24	18 x 26	20 x 26	20 x 26
Coupled wheel dia (ft – in)	6 – 0	6 – 6	5 – 0	5 – 9	4 – 9	4 – 9
Coupled wheel base (ft – in)	9 – 6	10 – 0	7 – 6	7 – 6	19 – 0	19 – 0
Bogie wheel dia (ft – in)	3 – 6	3 – 6	3 – 6	3 – 6	–	–
Bogie wheel base (ft – in)	6 – 6	6 – 6	5 – 6	6 – 0	–	–
Total wheel base of engine (ft – in)	22 – 3	23 – 9	22 – 0	c23 – 9	19 – 0	19 – 0
Height to C L of boiler (ft – in)	7 – 9	8 – 6	7 – 3	7 – 6	8 – 0	8 – 0
Max. external dia of boiler (ft – in)	4 – 6¾	4 – 9¾	4 – 1	4 – 6¼	4 – 11 5/8	5 – 0¾
Length between tubeplates (ft – in)	10 – 9 7/8	11 – 4 5/8	10 – 7 3/8	10 – 9 7/8	14 – 10 5/8	13 – 4 5/8
Length of outer firebox (ft – in)	7 – 9	8 – 3	5 – 9	6 – 4	8 – 3	8 – 3
Tubes No. & dia (in)	258 – 1¾	233 – 2	202 – 1¾	214 – 1¾	256 – 2	256 – 2
Heating surface (sq ft): tubes	1280	1390	979	1061	1995	1794
firebox	125	145	106	117	155	155
cross tubes	–	215	–	–	180	186
Grate area (sq ft)	25	27	18	20.37	27	27
Boiler pressure (lb/sq in)	175	175	170	175	175	175
Tractive effort @ 85% (lb)	18,384	17,900	16,704	18,160	27,140	27,140
Coal (tons)	–	–	1¾	2	–	–
Water (gal)	–	–	1200	1600	–	–

Notes:
1. All engines were provided with Stephenson valve gear.
2. Only one design, the larger tank, has any weights shown and these were 33 tons 15 cwt adhesion and 54 tons 0 cwt total in working order.

APPENDIX 11

HR ALLOCATION OF ENGINES – Summer 1919

Wheel Arrangement	Class	Nos	Totals Class	Totals Shed
Perth				
4–6–0	Clan	49, 51, 52	3	
	Castle	28, 29, 35, 50, 58, 59, 147, 149	8	
	Superheater	77, 78	2	
	Big Goods	103, 106, 107, 109	4	
4–4–0	Small Ben	1, 17	2	
	Loch	122, 123, 127, 130	4	
0–6–0	Barney	18, 19, 138, 139	4	
0–6–4T	Banking Tank	42, 44	2	
0–6–0T	Scrap Tank	24	1	
4–4–0T	Jones Tank	58A, 59A	2	32
Inverness				
4–6–0	Clan	53	1	
	Castle	26, 27, 30, 140 to 146	10	
	Superheater	75, 76	2	
	Big Goods	104, 105, 108, 110 to 117	11	
4–4–0	No. 73	73, 74	2	
	Big Ben	60 to 65	6	
	Small Ben	2, 7, 10, 13, 15, 16, 38, 41, 47	9	
	Loch	70 to 72, 121, 124, 129, 131, 133	8	
	Clyde Bogie	76A to 78A, 80, 82	5	
	Lochgorm Bogie	74A, 75A	2	
0–6–0	Barney	20, 36, 136, 137	4	
0–6–0T	Scrap Tank	22, 23	2	
	Lochgorm Tank	57	1	
4–4–0T	Jones Tank	50A	1	
0–4–4T	Passenger Tank	46	1	45
Blair Atholl				
4–4–0	Small Ben	14	1	
	Strath	96 to 100	5	
0–6–4T	Banking Tank	39, 43, 66, 68, 69	5	11
Aberfeldy				
4–4–0T	Yankee Tank	102	1	1
Aviemore				
4–6–0	Castle	148	1	
4–4–0	Small Ben	4 to 6, 8, 11	5	
	Loch	119, 120, 126, 128, 132	5	
	Lochgorm Bogie	72A	1	
2–4–0	Glenbarry	35A	1	13
Keith				
4–4–0	Small Ben	12	1	1

Wheel Arrangement	Class	Nos	Totals Class	Totals Shed
Forres				
4–4–0	Small Ben	9	1	
	Strath	90, 92 to 94	4	
	Lochgorm Bogie	84A	1	
	Duke	67A	1	
2–4–0	18	27B	1	
0–6–4T	Banking Tank	31	1	
4–4–0T	Yankee Tank	52A	1	10
Fochabers				
0–4–4T	Passenger Tank	40	1	1
Burghead				
4–4–0T	Yankee Tank	54, 51A	2	2
Kingussie				
4–4–0	Loch	125	1	
	Clyde Bogie	81	1	2
Dingwall				
4–4–0	Small Ben	3	1	
	Sky Bogie	87, 88	2	
0–4–4T	Passenger Tank	25	1	4
Fortrose				
4–4–0T	Yankee Tank	101	1	1
Kyle of Lochalsh				
4–4–0	Skye Bogie	32 to 34, 48, 85, 86	6	6
Dornoch				
0–6–0T	Lochgorm Tank	56A	1	1
Helmsdale				
4–4–0	Strath	95	1	
0–6–0	Barney	134, 135	2	3
Thurso				
4–4–0	Clyde Bogie	79	1	1
Wick				
4–4–0	Strath	89, 91	2	
	Clyde Bogie	83	1	
2–4–0	36	37	1	
0–6–0T	Lochgorm Tank	49A	1	
2–4–0T	Special Tank	118	1	6
Lybster				
0–4–4T	Passenger Tank	45	1	
	53 rebt.	53A	1	2
Tain				
0–6–0	Barney	21, 55	2	2

Note: 4–4–0 Skye Bogie No. 70A unaccounted for.

APPENDIX 12

LMS NORTHERN DIVISION (HIGHLAND SECTION)
ALLOCATION OF ENGINES
November 1935

Wheel arrange-ment	*Coy*	*Class*	*Nos*	*Totals Class*	*Totals Shed*
Perth North					
4–6–0	LMS	5P5F	5021 to 6	6	
	HR/CR	River	14756 to 61	6	
	HR	Castle	14678/84/90/91	4	
2–6–0	LMS	Crab	2800/01/03 to 06/08, 13102/09	9	
4–4–0	HR	Loch	14382	1	
0–6–0	LMS	4F	4312 to 15/18	5	
0–6–0T	LMS	3F	7329	1	32
Blair Atholl					
4–4–0	HR	Small Ben	14397, 14410	2	
	HR	Loch	14384, 14392	2	
0–6–4T	HR	Banking Tank	15306	1	
0–6–2T	GSW	Whitelegg Tank	16902	1	6
Aberfeldy					
0–4–4T	CR	439	15215	1	1
Inverness					
4–6–0	LMS	5P5F	5008 to 17/28, 29 and 5028 on loan	13	
	HR	Clan	14766	1	
	HR	Castle	14675/76/79/85/89/92	6	
	HR	Superheater	17952/55 to 57	4	
	HR	Big Goods	17917/23/26/27/29	5	
4–4–0	HR	Small Ben	14404/11	2	
	HR	Loch	14381/86/94/95	4	
0–6–0	HR	Barney	17698, 17700/02	3	
	CR	812	17606 on loan	1	
0–6–0T	LMS	3F	16416, 16624	2	
	CR	782	16291	1	
0–4–4T	CR	439	15199, 15226	2	
	CR	171	15103	1	
0–4–2ST	CR	Killin Tank	15001	1	
0–4–0ST	CR	264	16011	1	47
Dingwall					
4–6–0	HR	Superheater	17953/54	2	
0–6–0	HR	Barney	17693	1	3
Fortrose					
4–4–0	HR	Small Ben	14412	1	1
Fort George					
4–4–0	HR	Small Ben	14405	1	1
Kyle of Lochlash					
4–6–0	HR	Superheater	17950/51	2	
4–4–0	HR	Small Ben	14416	1	3
Tain					
4–6–0	HR	Big Goods	17930	1	
0–6–0	HR	Barney	17699	1	
4–4–0	HR	Loch	14390	1	3

Wheel arrange-ment	*Coy*	*Class*	*Nos*	*Totals Class*	*Totals Shed*
Dornoch					
0–4–4T	HR	Passenger Tank	15054	1	1
Helmsdale					
4–4–0	HR	Small Ben	14403/09	2	
0–6–0	HR	Barney	17695/97, 17703	3	5
Lybster					
0–4–4T	HR	Passenger Tank	15051	1	1
Wick					
4–6–0	HR	Castle	14681/83	2	
0–6–0	HR	Barney	17694, 17701	2	
0–4–4T	HR	Passenger Tank	15053	1	5
Thurso					
4–4–0	HR	Small Ben	14415	1	1
Aviemore					
4–6–0	HR	Castle	14677/82	2	
	HR	Big Goods	17920/25	2	
4–4–0	HR	73	14522	1	
	HR	Big Ben	14417/19	2	
	HR	Loch	14379/85	2	
0–6–0	HR	Barney	17696	1	10
Forres					
4–4–0	HR	Big Ben	14422	1	
	HR	Small Ben	14398 to 14402/06	6	
	HR	Loch	14380/91	2	
0–6–4T	HR	Banking Tank	15300	1	
0–6–0T	LMS	3F	16623	1	11
Keith					
4–4–0	HR	Small Ben	14408	1	
0–6–0	HR	Barney	17704	1	2
Burghead					
0–6–0T	LMS	3F	16415	1	1

Also the following HR locomotives were stationed off the Highland Section:—

Wheel arrange-ment	*Coy*	*Class*	*Nos*	*Totals Class*	*Totals Shed*
Stirling					
4–6–0		Clan	14762/65	2	
Oban					
4–6–0		Clan	14764	1	
St. Rollox					
4–6–0		Clan	14763/67 to 69	4	
		Castle	14686 (on loan)	1	8

APPENDIX 13

LMS NORTHERN DIVISION (HIGHLAND SECTION)
ALLOCATION OF ENGINES
April 1944

Wheel arrange-ment	*Coy*	*Class*	*Nos*	*Totals Class*	*Totals Shed*
Perth					
4–6–0	LMS	5P5F	5036/81/82/85 to 87, 5125/63 to 68/70 to 5175/94, 5241/51/66, 5309/57/65/66/89, 5443/52/56 to 67/69/70/72 to 75	48	
4–4–0	LMS	Compound	921 to 24/38/39, 1125/27/33/55/83	11	
	CR	Pickersgill II	14482/89/93/99, 14500 to 03	8	
	CR	Pickersgill I	14468/69/76	3	
	CR	139	14447/48/58	3	
2–8–0	LMS	8F	8311 to 13/18 to 20/36/37/39/40, 8623/47	12	
0–6–0	LMS	4F	4187/93, 4234/51/98, 4314/17/22/28	9	
	CR	Std. Goods	17339/74/97	3	
0–6–0T	CR	782	16246/90, 16328/31/47/52	6	
0–4–4T	CR	439	15159 to 61/63/68/71/75/76/87, 15208/09/13/15/16/18/20/29/38	18	
	CR	92	15144	1	122

Note: On the opening of the reconstructed Perth (South) depot in May 1938 the LMS closed Perth (North) and transferred all engines to the new depot and those listed above were available for duties on the ex Caledonian lines as well as the Highland. For instance only the very occasional compound found its way on Highland territory. In addition engines might be shedded out at sub-sheds, but these are not shown.

Also the following HR locomotives were stationed off the Highland Section:—

Wheel arrange-ment	*Coy*	*Class*	*Nos*	*Totals Class*	*Totals Shed*
Ayr					
4–6–0	HR/CR	River	14758/60	2	

Wheel arrange-ment	*Coy*	*Class*	*Nos*	*Totals Class*	*Totals Shed*
Inverness					
4–6–0	LMS	5P5F	5005/07/09 to 12/14 to 16/18/53/66, 5083/84/90/98, 5120 to 24/59 to 61/92, 5213, 5319/20/60/61, 5476 to 79	34	
	HR	Clan	14762 to 65/67/68	6	
	HR	Superheater	17950 to 7	8	
	HR	Castle	14681/85/86/89	4	
4–4–0	CR	Dunalastair III	14340/48	2	
	CR	Dunalastair II	14331	1	
	HR	Small Ben	14397, 14400/01/03 to 05/08 to 10/12/15/16	12	
	HR	Loch	14392	1	
0–6–0	LMS	4F	4258	1	
	CR	Std. Goods	17330	1	
	HR	Barney	17693 to 5/97, 17702/03	6	
0–6–0T	LMS	3F	7333, 7541	2	
	CR	782	16291/93/99, 16341	4	
0–4–4T	CR	439	15199	1	
	CR	171	15103	1	
	HR	Passenger Tank	15051/53/54	3	
0–4–2ST	CR	Killin Tank	15001	1	
0–4–2T	LBSC	D1	SR Nos. 2358, 2699	2	
0–4–0ST	CR	264	16011	1	92
Aviemore					
4–6–0	LMS	5P5F	5136/8	2	
	HR	Castle	14690/92	2	
4–4–0	CR	Dunalastair III	14338	1	
	HR	Small Ben	14398/99	2	
	HR	Loch	14379	1	
0–6–0	HR	Barney	17699, 17700	2	10
Forres					
4–6–0	HR	Castle	14678	1	
4–4–0	CR	Dunalastair III	14337, 14434	2	
	CR	Dunalastair II	14332, 14333	2	
	HR	Small Ben	14406	1	
	HR	Loch	14385	1	
0–6–0	HR	Barney	17696/98, 17704	3	
0–6–0T	CR	782	16301	1	11

APPENDIX 14

Class	Nos	Date built	Built by	Order No.	Cost per engine £
Raigmore (I)	1 & 2	'55	Hawthorn		2,453
	3	'56	Hawthorn		2,480
	4	'57	Hawthorn		2,610
Seafield	5 to 11	'58	Hawthorn		2,776
Belladrum	12 & 13	'62	Hawthorn		2,525
No. 14	14 & 15	'62	Hawthorn		2,775
No. 16	16	'59	Neilson	422	
No. 17	17	'63	Hawthorn		1,475
No. 18	18 to 27	'63	Sharp Stewart	433	2,825
Glenbarry	28 & 29	'63	Hawthorn		2,900
	30 to 35	'63	Neilson	966 & 972	2,770
	46 to 55	'64	Neilson	1054 & 1064	2,880
No. 36	36 to 45	'64	Sharp Stewart	459	3,000
Lochgorm tank	56, 57 & 16	'69 to '74	Lochgorm	–	1,250
No. 2	2	'71	Lochgorm	–	2,500
Duke	60 to 69	'74	Dübs	714	3,480
Lochgorm bogie	4	'76	Lochgorm	–	3,475
	71 to 75	'82 to '86	Lochgorm	–	3,100
	84	'88	Lochgorm	–	2,800
Raigmore (II)	3 & 1	'77	Lochgorm	–	2,775
Jones tank	58, 59 & 17	'78 to '79	Lochgorm	–	1,900
Skye bogie	70	'82	Lochgorm	–	3,100
	85 to 88	'92 to '95	Lochgorm	–	3,480
	5 to 7 & 48	'97 to '01	Lochgorm	–	2,342
Clyde bogie	76 to 83	'86	Clyde Loco	1	2,395
No. 13	13	'90	Lochgorm	–	1,214
Strath	89 to 100	'92	Neilson	693	2,502
No. 101	101 & 102	'92	Dübs	2778	1,500
Yankee tank	11, 14 & 15	'93	Dübs	3077	1,600
Big Goods	103 to 117	'94	Sharp Stewart	1039	2,795
Loch	119 to 133	'96	Dübs	3392	2,940
	70 to 72	'17	NB Loco	L667	4,541
Small Ben	1 to 8	'98 to '99	Dübs	3685	3,025
	9 to 17	'99 to '01	Lochgorm	–	2,494
	38, 41, 47	'06	NB Loco	L177	3,459
Barney	134 to 139	'00	Dübs	3842	2,750
	18 to 21	'02	Dübs	4240	3,140
	36 & 55	'07	NB Loco	L227	3,475
Castle I	140 to 145	'00	Dübs	3848	4,125
	146 to 149	'02	Dübs	4244	3,865
	30 & 35	'10 to '11	NB Loco	L365	3,830
Scrap tank	22 to 24	'03 to '04	Lochgorm	–	1,643
Passenger tank	25, 40, 45	'05	Lochgorm	–	1,289
	46	'06	Lochgorm	–	1,302
Big Ben	61, 63, 66, 68	'08	NB Loco	L265	3,900
	60 & 62	'09	NB Loco	L335	3,725
Banking tank	39, 64, 65, 69	'09	NB Loco	L336	3,005
	29, 31, 42, 44	'10 to '12	NB Loco	L366	2,980
Castle II	26 to 28, 43	'13	NB Loco	L527	4,193
River	70 to (75)	'15	Hawthorn Leslie	–	4,920
No. 73	73 & 74	'16	Hawthorn Leslie	–	5,363
Castle III	50, 58, 59	'17	NB Loco	L668	5,436
Superheated Goods	75 to 78	'18	Hawthorn Leslie	–	6,977
	79 to 82	'19	Hawthorn Leslie	–	10,766 to 10,810
Clan	49, 51 to 53	'19	Hawthorn Leslie	–	9,071 to 9,153
	54 to 57	'21	Hawthorn Leslie	–	11,166

APPENDIX 15

LOCOMOTIVE CLASSES AND CLASSIFICATIONS

Class name	Class letter of 1901	LMS power classification pre 1928	post 1927	Other unofficial descriptions
Castle	A	3	3P	
Loch	B	2	2P	
Ben	C	2	2P	Small Ben
Strath	D	1	1P	Glen
Bruce	E	1	(1P)	Clyde Bogie
Duke	F	—	—	
Glenbarry	G	—	—	
Raigmore (II)	H	—	—	
Big Goods	I	(4)	4F	Jones Goods
Drummond Goods	K	(3)	3F	Barney
Skye Bogie	L	1	(1P)	
Medium Goods	M	—	—	
Small Goods	N	—	—	
Jones tank	O	Uncl.	—	
Yankee tank	P	Uncl.	—	
Lochgorm tank	R	Uncl.	2F	
Strathpeffer tank	S	Uncl.	—	
Special tank	T	—	—	
Needlefield tank	U	—	—	
New Ben	U ('08)	2	2P	Big Ben
Shunting tank	V ('03)	(2)	2F	Scrap tank
Passenger tank	W ('05)	Uncl.	1P	
Banking tank	X ('09)	4	4P	Struan banker or Big Pug
River	—	4	4P	
Nos 73 & 74	—	3	3P	
Superheated Goods	—	(4)	4F	Superheater or Clan Goods
Clan	—	4	4P	

Note: LMS power classifications in brackets ( ) were not actually applied to the cabsides.

ACKNOWLEDGEMENTS

The revising author is grateful to the many organisations and individuals who have generously afforded him assistance in numerous ways during his task of preparing the manuscript for the second edition. Reference has been made to documents in the custody of the Mitchell Library, Glasgow; the National Library of Scotland, Edinburgh; the National Railway Museum, York; the Science Museum, London and the Scottish Record Office, Edinburgh at all of which he was kindly received. Further material, comment and support has been generously provided by Messrs. E N Bellass, R B Constant, A G Dunbar, E McKenna and J W P Rowledge.

Not all the photographs included in the first edition were available for this edition, but the old and new plates are attributable to the following:—

E N Bellass collection: 139 and 150.

W E Boyd collection: 85, 100, 121, 134 and 145.

British Rail: 2, 6, 14, 59, 70, 75, 102, 112, 118, 125, 128, 146 and 147.

H C Casserley: 3, 5, 24, 36, 40, 43, 46, 50, 55, 57, 58, 62, 63, 68, 69, 79, 80, 81, 83, 89, 91, 97, 99, 105, 110, 113, 117, 122, 127, 130, 131, 132, 142, 144, 152, 153 and 154.

H C Casserley collection: 78 and 140

R B Constant collection: 35 and 76.

J M Craig: 126, 137 and 149.

A W Croughton: 20.

A G Ellis collection: 4, 9, 15, 17, 26, 34, 44, 60, 65, 93, 94, 98, 120, 138, 141, 143, 151 and 155.

M Golder collection: 82.

Inverness Museum: 74 and 115.

G E Langmuir: 123.

Locomotive Publishing Co. (courtesy Ian Allan Ltd): 7, 12, 19, 21, 22, 27, 29, 30, 38, 42, 48, 66, 86, 87, 96 and 103.

Locomotive Publishing Co. (F Moore): 18, 32, 47, 51, 52, 54, 116 and 118.

LCGB Ken Nunn collection: 136.

K H Leech collection: 53 and 77.

J F McEwan collection: 1 and 10.

North British Locomotive Co. (courtesy Mitchell Library): 16 and 99.

Photomatic: 37, 133 and 135.

W O Steel collection (courtesy R J Essery): 8, 11, 13, 25 and 56.

P Tatlow: 72, 156 and 157.

Wakefields: 108.

The remainder being from the revising author's collection.

The drawings too have been gleaned from a variety of sources and acknowledgement is made for the following figures:—

E N Bellass: 8, 9, 27, 34, 35, 42, 44, 45 and 46.

H T Buckle (courtesy R B Constant): 15, 16 and 18.

K H Leech: 26 and 39.

North British Locomotive Co. (courtesy British Rail and Mitchell Library): 32, 33, 38 and 41.

L Ward: 13, 14, 19, 20, 23, 24, 25, 29 and 30.

The others being by the revising author.

In conclusion thanks are due to Marion for typing the manuscript without complaint, and my wife and two sons for assistance proof reading.

INDEX

Note: *The principal entries for a locomotive class are those shown in italics*

The three classes of Highland engines on shed at Aviemore on 9th April, 1946 are two 4–4–0s No. 14398 ***Ben Alder*** and No. 14379 ***Loch Insh*** both reboilered with Caley boilers and a 4–6–0 No. 14690 ***Dalcross Castle*** of the second series.

H.C. Casserley